THE BAFFLED PARENT'S GUIDE TO
COACHING YOUTH
SOCCER

THE BAFFLED PARENT'S

GUIDE TO

COACHING YOUTH
SOCCER

Bobby Clark

Head Coach, Stanford University Men's Team

With Nomad Communications
Norwich, Vermont

Ragged Mountain Press/McGraw-Hill

Camden, Maine • New York • San Francisco • Washington, D.C. • Auckland
Bogotá • Caracas • Lisbon • London • Madrid • Mexico City • Milan • Montreal
New Delhi • San Juan • Singapore • Sydney • Tokyo • Toronto

To all the kids who've ever played
for Upper Valley Lightning Soccer.

Ragged Mountain Press

*A Division of The **McGraw·Hill** Companies*

10 9 8 7 6 5 4 3 2 1

Library of Congress Cataloging-in-Publication Data
Clark, Bobby (Robert Brown)
    The baffled parent's guide to coaching youth soccer / Bobby Clark.
       p.   cm.
    Includes index.
    ISBN 0-07-134608-2
    1. Soccer for children—Coaching.   I. Title.
    GV943.8.C53   1999
    796.334'07'7—dc21   99-30450
                                    CIP

Questions regarding the content of this book should be addressed to
Ragged Mountain Press
P.O. Box 220
Camden, ME 04843
http://www.raggedmountainpress.com

Questions regarding the ordering of this book should be addressed to
The McGraw-Hill Companies
Customer Service Department
P.O. Box 547
Blacklick, OH 43004
Retail customers: 1-800-262-4729
Bookstores: 1-800-722-4726

This book is printed on 70-lb. Citation
Printed by Quebecor Printing, Fairfield PA
Design by Carol Gillette
Production by Eugenie S. Delaney and Dan Kirchoff
Edited by Tom McCarthy, Alex Barnett, and Jane M. Curran
Unless otherwise specified, photography by Mark Austin-Washburn

Contents

Foreword

Whenever I am asked to speak to parents at various soccer clinics, I am usually introduced as the head coach of the Chicago Fire. Although that sounds nice and might impress people, I always remind everyone that I have three soccer-playing children and have been faced with the challenge of coaching their youth teams on many occasions. I guess it is a little like running a good birthday party. Will the party be organized and a positive experience for everyone, including the birthday boy or girl, and the parents? Will the kids enjoy themselves and want to come back next time?

It really doesn't matter that I coach the Fire. Understanding the game of soccer helps, but it's far more important that I have a way with kids. Parents should understand this idea very well. Indeed, it's exactly what happens with all our children in their elementary school classrooms: *all* teachers know the material, but only the very special ones bring their classrooms to life day after day.

The same is true in soccer. I have been so fortunate to share the game with a few extraordinary individuals who are great with kids and love soccer. One of the best is Bobby Clark. Bobby's credentials—coaching in Zimbabwe and New Zealand as well as at two prestigious universities, Dartmouth and Stanford—are top-notch. But his credentials don't tell the whole story of Bobby's success. The many players who have come in contact with Bobby over the years know the real story: they would remember that Bobby's love of soccer and total enthusiasm made soccer fun and exciting for them. They would never forget the way Bobby Clark brought the game to life for them.

Coaching Youth Soccer: The Baffled Parent's Guide won't magically turn all our soccer parents into Bobby Clarks. It will, however, give all of you a wonderful opportunity to share the game with him. Best of all, it will inspire you and fill you with ideas to provide the type of positive soccer experience for your players that Bobby Clark has always given his players. Best of luck.

Bob Bradley
Head Coach, Chicago Fire, Major League Soccer
Assistant Coach, U.S. Men's National Soccer Team
Former Head Soccer Coach, Princeton University

Preface: Fitba' Is King

Most of my early soccer—or *fitba'*, the local slang for football—was played away from adult interference. In Glasgow, fitba' was king and everyone played. That was why I thought I went to school—so that I could play soccer on the playground before school, at morning break, at lunchtime, and at afternoon break. We played these games with a tennis ball. To think back, it must have been a fascinating sight to see four or five different minigames crisscrossing the tarmac playground all at the same time. Games were usually governed by class, and each had its own goal made up of a chalk mark on the wall.

Upon coming home after school I played more football. This time it would be out on the spare bit of grass in the neighborhood. We would put our jackets down as goals, and the games would begin. The games would vary depending on how many mates turned up—we'd play anything from one-on-one dribbling and heading games right up to small-sided games. These were great times and were very much the romantic period of my development. My friends and I pretended we were the heroes of our day and imitated what these players did on the field, just as young players today try to imitate Eddie Lewis, Brian McBride, Mia Hamm, or Cobi Jones. Even now as a coach, I still love to give a good picture so that kids can really immerse themselves in the game. When I was a younger coach, I was able to supply these pictures myself, but now as an older coach, I love to have young vibrant assistants who can provide meaningful actions the kids can imitate.

I didn't play organized soccer until I played for my school Under-12 team. There we trained twice a week, and that was the first time I came under adult supervision. We had two adult coaches—one was our teacher, Mr. McNaught, and the other was Jimmy Rough, a former pro. Even then, we didn't have serious coaching but plenty of healthy, controlled competition in small-sided games. I rarely played 11-on-11 games.

After 7th grade I went to secondary school, as was the norm in Scotland, and Glasgow High School had only a rugby team. Suddenly I was playing rugby in the morning and then playing soccer for a club team in the afternoon. Club teams in Scotland in those days began at age 16, so as a 12-year-old I found myself playing at the U-16 level. It was fun for me to find a way to compete against older players. I wasn't going to dominate these early matches physically, so I learned that I had to develop my soccer skills if I was going to compete with them. As the years progressed and I developed physically, my role changed. While this is very different from today's strictly defined age-group soccer, I always felt being the youngest player on the team initially allowed me to learn from older players. By the time I was 15, I was playing on the youth team for Queens Park Football Club (FC), a Scottish 2nd Division club. By my senior year in high school,

I was playing for their first team in the Scottish 2nd Division. I never thought too much about it at the time, but playing up always kept me finding ways to compete by being skillful rather than being physical.

When I was 19, I signed full professional forms for Aberdeen FC in the Scottish Premier League. I still had two years left at Jordanhill College, where I was studying Physical Education, but I had it written into my contract that the team would allow me to finish my degree. I was always conscious of finishing my education, although this was at a time when most of my fellow professionals at Aberdeen had left school at 15 and had gone straight into playing soccer for a living. I will always be indebted to Jordanhill for the guidance of so many fine lecturers.

Both of Scotland's two most recent national coaches, Andy Roxburgh and Craig Brown, are graduates of Jordanhill from around the same era. We were all lucky to be indoctrinated with a teaching philosophy that encouraged us to teach through games and to make our players think and be creative. We tried to put the youngsters into situations where *they* had to find the answers. We called it the *discovery method,* and I still use it today, even with my college players. Before a match I will tell them the way I feel the opposition will play, and then I'll ask my players how they think we should approach the game. If I have prepared them well over the years, then we will all be on the same wavelength, and the players should see the answer to that question the same way I do. I like this approach because the players feel that they know what the answer is and have contributed to solving the problem. I usually suggest a couple of scenarios, and they have to come up with the answers. That is one of the things that separates soccer from the other American sports. Since we don't call time-outs, the players need to be prepared so that when different situations arise during a game, they can work out solutions together. That for me is one of the most fascinating challenges of coaching at the top level.

I played with Aberdeen for 17 years. I played 696 matches on their first team, started 17 times for the full Scottish national team, and was lucky enough to win every domestic trophy in Scotland. It was during this time that I learned that although these moments were highlights, the real fun was in *trying* to win. Winning itself was empty. It was all the preparation, the tough times, the competition, and the people that made it all so very worthwhile. I realized that without question, it was the journey that was fun, not the destination.

From Player to Coach

I was fortunate enough throughout my time with Aberdeen to spend most afternoons teaching physical education in local high schools in the Aberdeen area. Since my job as a professional soccer player mainly required that I train in the mornings, I taught sports in the afternoons. Most players did nothing but play soccer, but I always felt that I did not want to waste my

Bobby Clark: *Coaching* is simply another word for *teaching*, so make it enjoyable.

training as a teacher, plus I enjoyed the diversion from the pro soccer world in my work with local kids. I felt I was putting something back into the community, but in fact the experience I gained would help my management skills once I seriously began to coach for a living. Let's face it: *coaching* is simply another word for *teaching*.

My soccer coaching really took off in earnest in my 13th season with Aberdeen, when Len Taylor and I took over the task of setting up the club's youth program, which was aimed at identifying and developing the local youth players in the northeast of Scotland. This was a fantastic five-year period that allowed me to work with the area's top players even though I was still playing for the club. It also gave me the opportunity to work closely with Alex Ferguson, now the Manchester United coach, as he was the head coach with Aberdeen through four of these years. Alex, as history has shown, is a tremendous coach, and many of the young players who came through our youth program at that time went on to play on the first team and, in my opinion, helped set up one of the best periods the club has ever enjoyed. Six players who graduated onto the senior team via that program were on the squad that brought the European Cup Winners Cup to Aberdeen when they beat Real Madrid in the cup final in 1983.

At the time Aberdeen was winning European glory, I had left the club and was coaching Highlanders FC in Bulawayo, Zimbabwe. Soccer had taken me to Africa thanks to my college lecturer, Roy Small, who also doubled as a coach and lecturer for the Federation Internationale de Football Association (FIFA). My wife and family had a wonderful year in Africa, and I learned that you do not need great equipment to be a great soccer player. Street football abounds in Africa. The young players seem to be constantly involved in games on dust-strewn streets, playing in bare feet and with a ball made up of tied rags. There were no adults in sight, and the game was once again the teacher.

On my return from Africa, I had offers to go into the Scottish game or go back for a further three years to my Zimbabwe club. Out of the blue, Hubert Vogelsinger, a former Yale coach and American soccer camp veteran called, suggesting that I would be well-suited to coaching at the college level in the United States. To be honest, I had never thought of this avenue, but I soon saw college coaching as an ideal way to use both my teaching skills and my knowledge of soccer. I applied to Dartmouth and enjoyed a fabulously happy nine years as soccer coach in Hanover, New Hampshire. That was a great time, since in addition to coaching at the college level, I took over and ran the local Upper Valley Lightning youth soccer program. My three children—Tommy, Jenni, and Jamie—all grew up with the help of Lightning soccer. It was fabulous to observe my own kids and their friends throughout those nine years.

Soccer has always been an enormous part of my life. I often joke that I have yet to work for a living—as long as I can remember I have always been paid for doing my hobby!

Introduction

So, you're a Baffled Parent.

You thought you were going to drop off your daughter at the rec department for a meeting on the upcoming soccer season and maybe stand in the background until the teams were picked. But before you could hide, you found yourself "appointed" coach of one of the teams, though "captured" might be more appropriate. Now you're in for it. You've never coached anything, let alone something that looks as chaotic as soccer. You never even *played* soccer, for that matter.

Don't worry, help is at hand.

This book is designed to help any coach have a successful season—and by successful I don't mean more wins than losses. The advice and games here are aimed at helping you teach 6- to 12-year-old boys and girls the basics of soccer, sportsmanship, teamwork, and, above all else, the fun and rewards of the game.

No book hoping to offer such advice will work unless it recognizes the differences, sometimes quite marked, in your players' abilities and responses to coaching—though most everyone reacts positively to encouragement and praise. I'll show you how to deal with this mix. Some kids are natural athletes, some aren't. Some kids may come to the first practice knowing more about the game than you. Others won't have a clue. Some will be anxious to learn, while others will be nervous about playing. Some won't be able to sit still or stop talking; others will sit quietly in the background. Girls, especially as they become older, might respond quite differently to criticism and instruction. I recognize this and give you advice on dealing with such issues throughout the book.

How to Use This Book

Coaching Youth Soccer: The Baffled Parent's Guide is a grab bag of soccer skills, teaching games and drills, and coaching techniques. The book is designed so novice and experienced coaches alike can teach their players—and perhaps themselves—the basics of good soccer. Need to brush up on the very basics of the game? Start with chapter 2, which outlines the rules of the game. Chapter 4, Essential Skills, teaches fundamental skills such as dribbling, passing and receiving, and shooting, and introduces the positions and tactics that are the building blocks of full-field play. Afraid the kids will ignore you—or eat you alive? Start with chapter 1, Creating an Atmosphere of Good Habits. What if you can't even organize your desk, let alone a soccer season? Chapter 3, Setting Up the Season, will start you off on the right foot. But what about the practice itself? Chapter 5 provides a template for a successful practice, and chapter 6 contains five sample practices, from beginner to advanced, with every blank filled in. Chapter 7, Game Time, will quiet the butterflies in your stomach and help your team approach competition with confidence, excitement, and respect, and chapter 8 addresses issues that might arise with parents or with coed teams. When you and your players are ready for a change or a new challenge, the dozens of games and drills described in chapter 9 will allow almost limitless variations.

Drills and games are numbered consecutively from 1 to 57 in chapter 9. When these games and drills are discussed elsewhere in the book, their numbers are provided for ease of reference.

Throughout the book you'll find helpful question-and-answer sections dealing with hard-to-handle situations that could come up during the season, and useful sidebars to ease your anxieties. You'll also find a detailed index to locate advice on specific problems, a glossary of soccer terms, a list of resources, and diagrams of referee signals.

Remember, one size does not fit all. You'll have to be able to adapt to the many, sometimes conflicting, demands placed on you. The tools to help are right here.

A Word on Coaching Style

While the games and techniques I've provided here have all worked for me for years, they fit *my* coaching style. A lot of my drills and games are set up as minicompetitions with winners and losers. Soccer is a competitive sport, and that's why most of the kids are playing it. I like to give little forfeits to the losers, like doing a few push-ups. These forfeits are always easy and meant to be fun little penalties. They are never meant to be punishments or negative in any way. I've found that they encourage the competitive aspect of practice and are great motivators. I especially enjoy games in which I, the coach, am subject to the same forfeit if the kids beat me by some standard—and I've found most kids enjoy the sight of the coach doing push-ups. However, if you feel the kids you are coaching are too young, or you just don't like "consequences," it's completely up to you. Choose what feels comfortable and leave the rest.

One good coach might be ebullient, another calm and quiet. There's no one right coaching style, but there are wrong ones. If you can keep your temper, never disparage the players or the referees, seek constantly to teach and encourage, and finish the season with improved players who enjoy the game and each other—then I don't need to see your won-loss record to know you're a good coach.

Remember that your goal is to make the soccer experience fun for your players. This is a time when kids should learn to work as a team while having a great time. As their coach, you are an important role model with an opportunity to teach this group of children many life lessons, in addition to sport-specific skills: to respect each other as individuals; to work together as a team; to view competition, both winning and losing, as part of the overall experience rather than an end in itself; and, above all, to have fun while discovering the skills of a game they can enjoy for a lifetime. These are all lessons you can help them learn, and you'll be surprised at what you can learn in the process.

Whatever your coaching credentials, your greatest responsibility is to give each team member a positive learning experience while teaching them some skills and helping them be the best individuals and teammates they can be. You can do it.

There are five keys to being a good coach:

Remember the Scouting motto: always be prepared. Every time you walk out onto the field, have a plan for what you want to accomplish during practice that day. Know what games and drills you'll work on and how long you want to spend on each one. Make sure that you are familiar enough with what you plan to do so that you can present it clearly. By organizing your thoughts and preparing a practice plan ahead of time, you'll keep the kids moving, interested, and learning.

On the other hand, be flexible: if it isn't working, do something else. You don't have to be a psychiatrist to judge when kids are motivated and having fun, and when they are bored. You can have a great practice plan on paper, but if for some reason it's not going well, be ready to change your plan and move on to something else.

Good words go a long way: keep it positive. Everyone loves praise and encouragement. Make sure that one of your cardinal rules is that the coach is the only person *ever* to criticize a player—and then only in a positive, constructive way. Kids should never criticize other kids. And remember that kids never can hear enough: "Great job," "Nice try," "Good work." Positive encouragement is vital to a positive experience.

Keep your energy level high. You need to match the energy level of the kids you'll be coaching and to show excitement and enthusiasm about the game, every time, all the time. Psych yourself up before each practice so that you are excited and energized from the moment you step onto the field. Your players will feed off of your energy, and everyone will have a better practice because of it.

Keep your eyes open and get to know your team. One of the best ways to learn to coach your team effectively is to observe. Watch your players carefully; get to know their personalities. You'll learn a lot just by watching how they react and interact with each other. And be sure to learn every player's name right away—they need the recognition and will respond positively to it.

Coaching Youth Soccer: The Baffled Parent's Guide

CHAPTER 1

Creating an Atmosphere of Good Habits

One of the most important things you can do as a coach is to instill good habits in your players. By teaching them to attend to the little things, such as getting to practice on time and coming with their soccer balls properly inflated and their equipment well cared for, they will start taking care of these details at the games—and perhaps in life as well. Players will learn to work as part of a team, and since this may well be the first time your players will be a part of a team, instilling good habits in them now lays a strong foundation for the future.

Establishing Yourself as Coach

Keep It Fun

You can help your players learn good habits only if they respect you and your position. Kids respond best to authority if they can have fun while they are learning what you expect of them, and if they are a part of the process. The best way to do this is to make everything a game. I've found that kids respond well to little forfeits that everyone enjoys. For example, if you want the team to come in from the field or to pick up all the cones, give them a challenge, and ask them how long it will take them to finish the job. They come up with the challenge for themselves: they may say they can pick up the cones in 30 seconds. Make it a contest: if they can get the cones in 25 seconds, they win, and you will do 10 push-ups. If you win, they do 10 push-ups. The task becomes a game, and you're a part of it—they can catch you the same as you can catch them. They are learning to take responsibility for their actions, and learning this valuable lesson can be done in a fun way.

Let Your Signal Be Their Guide

Your players will need to learn to listen to you and to respond to your signal. When you want them to listen, speak in a quiet voice—when you speak

Kids respond best to authority if they're having fun while they are learning what to expect from you.

in a loud voice, their volume will rise to meet your voice. Speak to them softly, or don't even speak at all—when someone is not paying attention and you stop speaking, your silence will get the message across. Then everyone refocuses on you, and you can carry on.

Set a Good Example

The coach has to set standards—if you expect your kids to play like a team, to pay attention, and to focus on the sport, your discipline has to be the best of everyone's. You have to be dressed to play, ready to play, and focused on what you are doing even more than your players.

Be Aware of the Environment around You

When you want your players to focus on you, be aware of other distractions—such as other practices or games. Position yourself and the demonstrations so that the kids are looking away from other distractions. You can repeatedly bring them in close around you, but this takes a lot of time. I'm a strong believer in keeping a good tempo during practice. Bring your players in close enough so they can hear you, but don't waste time stopping and bringing them in just to send them out again. If it's a strong wind, bring them in closer so they can hear, and if it's a low sun, be careful where you position yourself so they aren't looking into the sun to see you.

Assess Their Attention Span

You will need to learn how long your players can pay attention without getting bored or restless. The biggest mistake you can make is to do all the talking or demonstrating. I watched a camp in New Jersey many years ago. The head coach was working hard, and as the day wore on, the coach enjoyed doing the demonstrations more and more. It ended up that the kids were moving for about 30 seconds or so, and then the coach was demonstrating for 3 minutes, and it wasn't clear who was having a good time—the coach or the kids. The players are the ones who need the practice. Keep that in mind.

Drills to Promote Good Habits on the Field

Right from the beginning, on the first day of practice, you'll want to incorporate drills that promote good habits. These games are fun, and I use at least a couple of them in every practice to teach the kids to focus and really listen. Some of the drills are great for starting out practice, as a warm-up, whereas others can be mixed into your other games and drills.

Numbers Warm-Up

Give your players different exercises, each rhyming with a number. You say, "Number three," and they respond, "Down on one knee" while they go down on one knee. Or you say, "Number seven," and they respond, "Up to heaven," and kick the ball up high in the air. Inevitably you'll catch someone doing the wrong exercise to correspond to the number you gave, but as the season progresses, they'll remember the exercises that go with each number. You'll find that your kids are listening to you, and listening care-

A simple game like Do This, Do That teaches kids how to listen and how to focus on the coach.

fully. You're warming them up, they aren't talking, and they are tuned in, but they think they are playing a game—that's the key to having the kids listen and learn discipline.

Do This, Do That

Have the kids follow your lead when you say, "Do this," like touching their hands to their shoulders or head, or holding their arms straight out to the side or in front of themselves. There are lots of possible movements that you can incorporate into this game. But when you say, "Do that," players shouldn't follow your lead. This will get them paying attention to you, and you have a game going. Penalties need to be kept simple—lifting one knee to the chest (an "Irish" push-up), for example. This is one of my all-time favorite games. They can catch you, and you can catch them. Sometimes you should let them catch you making a wrong movement so the coach can be one of the players, too. The kids love it when the coach gets it wrong, and you'll have all eyes on you—they will focus on you, which is the whole point.

Last One In

The point of this drill is to teach your players to move quickly and with a purpose. When you want to have a group talk, call them around you. Say, "Last one in gets caught!" and give a little penalty.

Freeze!

During dribbling drills you can also encourage players to really pay attention by playing this game. When you say, "Stop!" or blow the whistle, have them all freeze. If anyone keeps moving, give a penalty. Tell them that good players are always in control of the ball. When you say, "Stop!" and the ball keeps rolling, that can also cause a forfeit. All this time you're getting players to concentrate.

Team Relays

Divide your players into teams for team relay races. Use the soccer field as your course, setting the length of the legs of the relay according to the ability level of your team members. When the last player of the first team finishes, that team sits down. As the other teams finish, they do the same thing, so that finished players aren't wandering all over the place after they finish—they are in straight lines sitting down. Organize the game so that the winning team isn't necessarily the first team finished, but the first team in, sitting down. Ten or fifteen minutes are plenty of time for this game.

Opposites

This game is designed to keep your players focused on your directions. Explain to your players that when you shout one instruction, they should do the opposite. Choose one set of activities, such as "heading and catching" or

About Forfeits

Little forfeits are a great way to keep all of my games competitive. But it's essential that you keep the penalties fun and easy—they should never be anything like a punishment. I give my forfeits names like Flying Scotsmen or Flying Irishmen, and they can be any silly movement that you wish to do—something funny, rather than hard. You come up with your own. I usually use Scotsmen, which fits into my character, and I have the kids doing a dance movement like the Highland fling. Irish push-ups are good for 10-year-olds, with the players doing push-ups from their knees. Or you can have them do a couple of jumps trying to hit their knees to their chest. Use your imagination.

Forfeits keep games competitive, but they should never be used for punishment. Keep it fun.

"pass and stop" each time you play this game, and then define what the activity and its opposite are.

This drill can be done with partners or with the entire group. Players form a circle around you. You throw a player the ball and shout one instruction, but she is to do the opposite action. For example, you throw the ball and shout, "Head," but what she should do is catch it. If you throw the ball and shout, "Catch," you want her to head it. If she gets it wrong, she has to run around the circle. This is a difficult game, and you'll find your players will be very focused and listening to you. Trick games like this will increase concentration and discipline.

Passing the Squeeze

This drill, a good one to do at the end of practice, calms down the team. Players come together in a circle, sit down, and hold the hands of the players on either side. One person starts by squeezing the hand of the person to his right (or to his left, if you want to go in that direction); that person squeezes the hand of the person to her right, and so on until the squeeze goes all the way around the circle. You time how quickly players can pass the squeeze. You can do this in two teams, too. This is a quiet drill, with players sitting still, but they are concentrating, having fun, and working like a team to accomplish the task. And you are giving them a rest, which is especially important for younger players.

Silent Drills

When your team is working on passing drills, add this element to the game. Have them do the passing drills without making a sound, so the players learn to read each other: when they are ready to pass and receive, and where they want the ball. They learn the discipline of observation and of communicating without shouting. Obviously, players need to communicate verbally, but sometimes it is important to be able to read other players' body language. One way to learn that is to play in silence.

Questions and Answers

Q. I have a couple of players who consistently talk when I'm talking. It's not loud or obnoxious, but they tend to whisper together when I'm trying to explain a skill or demonstrate something. How should I address this?

A. When a player is speaking out of turn, you don't need to stop the whole session to give them a reprimand. An easy way is to throw their name into whatever you're talking about. You can bring the person who is not paying attention, who is talking, or whatever back into the conversation. This is a nice way to bring them in. You can also use your assistant to help keep kids on track by saying, "Listen to the coach," or "Watch what we're doing." This makes players focus in nicely. Or you might ask them questions to bring them back into focus.

Q. I have one player on my team who seems to be here only because his parents want him to participate. He doesn't listen when I'm explaining a skill or demonstrating a drill, and he goofs off on the field. It's affecting the players around him, who start goofing off when he does. How do I get him to become more a part of the team without singling him out for discipline all the time?

A. The best solution to this problem is to keep the player who is goofing off involved in the explanations, demonstrations, and drills. Ask him to demonstrate, or ask him plenty of questions about the skills you're trying to teach, so that he doesn't have a chance to fool around. This also helps to make him feel like an important part of the team. If the player is disrupting everyone else's learning experience and good time, take him aside at the end of practice and tell him that he can't participate if he can't pay attention. Remember to keep your explanations and teaching short and to the point, since young kids have short attention spans. Also, look at your own coaching style. Are you talking too much? Kids need to be active and moving, and your coaching style needs to allow for that.

Q. I have a player who is consistently very late to practice. It's disruptive because I have to stop whatever I'm doing and explain everything all over again. I know it isn't really her fault because her parents drive her there, but how do I address it?

A. Since it's often not a child's fault when parents are responsible for driving her to and from practices, have the player do a small forfeit at the end of practice so that everyone knows you don't want people to come late, but that you aren't really punishing her. Make sure that it is quite clear at the beginning of the season that players are expected to get to practice on time, and explain what the consequences will be for being late. You may need to call the parents and help determine a solution to the problem—perhaps carpooling with a friend, for example. You may find that the child really doesn't want to be there, and so she purposely *is* late. The best way to solve the problem is to address it in a straightforward manner with the parents.

Q. A few of my players are much better than some of the others, and they have begun criticizing the less-skilled kids. I don't like it, but I can understand the better-skilled kids' frustration. How do I address this?

A. Address the people involved in the incident. Take them aside after practice individually, and stress that their team is like a chain, only as strong as the weakest link. Suggest to them that they could help strengthen the chain by using their better skills to teach and encourage the weaker players. Rather than making this a punishment for the better-skilled players, make them feel special and feel that they are doing something important by helping their teammates.

CHAPTER 2

Before Hitting the Field: Soccer in a Nutshell

This chapter is about the rules of soccer, and to be honest, when coaching kids I feel that the fewer rules you introduce, the better. *Especially* when kids are just learning. I am a great believer that the coach should know the rules, but I would stress that one of the great things about soccer is that there are relatively few rules to worry about.

When working with youngsters who are just starting out, I usually lay down two goals and little else. My instructions are simple: "Reds defend this goal, blues defend that goal. The goalie is the only person who can handle the ball"—and that's about it. I usually have an end line but rarely bother with a sideline. Throw-ins are just a complication that youngsters don't need at an early stage.

Manfred Schellscheidt, the Seton Hall University coach and longtime soccer guru, loves to play the Soccer Game that Never Ends. Manfred just has two small goals, two or three yards wide, no goalkeepers, and no end lines at all. Whenever the ball goes behind the goal, the game continues, with the first team to retrieve the ball keeping it. The only rule is that you can only score through the front of the goal. The game never stops!

My advice to you as a coach is *don't get caught up in the rules.* Certainly don't spend too much time worrying about them. Instead, spend your time playing and dealing with important things like dribbling, passing, and scoring goals . . . not worrying about offsides, indirect free kicks, and the like. Keep it *very* simple, and as the kids progress in ability and start to be involved in more serious competition, the rules will quite naturally acquire more importance and will take care of themselves.

I remember a certain tournament in Scotland for grade 7 and under, with 7 players on each side. I was refereeing, and one team was winning and clearly the stronger side. The result was never in doubt. I allowed a couple of little advantages for the weaker team. I was astounded by the reaction of the parents of the stronger team to these decisions. I certainly believe in bending rules to fit the ability level and making it an enjoyable experience for all the players. I believe that good coaches, parents, and referees share my feelings. When the kids grow up and are playing in the World Cup Final, the rules can be administered to the law. Mind you, even there the good referee always remembers the unwritten law of "common sense."

Soccer is perhaps the simplest team game ever invented. All you need is a ball and a piece of ground to play on, a couple of jackets for goals, and away you go. When we were kids, the first person to the park would juggle his ball. Once a friend joined in, there would be a heading or shooting game with plenty of shots and saves. When there were a few more of us, we would play "Three and In," where one player was the goalie and the other players were all dribbling and competing against each other to score. As soon as someone scored three goals he would become the new goalie, and the game would begin again. Once there were eight players we would play four-on-four—and the game would just keep growing.

The rules are so easy in these small unstructured games, and the players just lose themselves chasing the ball around. Soccer is all about running and kicking to begin with, but as the youngsters start to get a feel for the strategies of the game, it soon becomes apparent that it is a thinking person's game. It becomes more than just about running, but about where and when to run. It is fascinating to watch kids get a feeling for the game. One of the most important things to remember about coaching soccer is that the game is the best teacher. Coaches should keep the youngsters playing the game rather than running too many drills.

Remember, the game itself is the best teacher. Keep drills to a minimum and let the kids play.

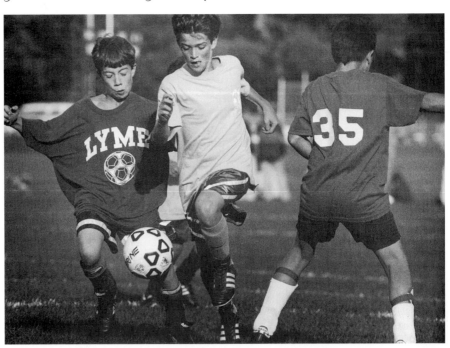

Following, you'll find the basics of soccer, from the number of players to rules and fundamental skills to offensive and defensive basics. Even if you start out knowing nothing about the game, this chapter will help you get your bearings.

How Many on a Team?

My strong recommendation for kids under 12 is to play no more than seven-on-seven soccer using half a full-sized field, for several reasons (for various ways to reduce the size of the field, see page 119). The first and most important reason is that the kids are there to have fun and learn the fundamentals of the game. You'll have kids of all ability levels on your team. Games of six-on-six or seven-on-seven allow young players to touch the ball more often, work on and hone passing and ball-handling skills, and learn to space themselves properly over the field. This smaller field setup also teaches kids to work as a team. Playing on a small field during practices, your players are learning the fundamental skills and are working on moving the ball down the field as a cohesive unit. When game day rolls around, the players are comfortable with each other on the field, and you can really start to coach them beyond reminding them to keep their heads up and to touch the ball with the proper part of the their feet.

With most players under age 12, an 11-on-11 game on a full-sized field defeats the purpose of learning basic skills and having fun. It's also much harder to coach. A siege mentality starts: there's one ball and twenty outfield players all fighting for a bit of it, and it's pretty hard to teach them to move the ball with purpose and to pass to each other. To succeed in a full-field game, the players will need good control and ball-handling skills and need to play with their heads up. On an average team, fewer than half of the players will have these skills honed, so the game breaks down. Fewer kids get to touch the ball—some kids in an 11-on-11 game never will. Playing on a field designed for adults means these young players run up to six miles a game—this can be too much for young kids.

Having said that however, the reality of youth soccer is that many recreational departments *do* have kids under age 12 playing 11-on-11 full-field soccer. Since that is the case, the most effective way to teach players good soccer skills for a full-field game is with set positions, or formations, that resemble three-on-two and three-on-one scrimmages. The key difference is that the players start to get a sense of how to move the ball from one end of the field to another.

Basic Rules

Rules for youngsters should be kept to a minimum. I am a great believer in small-sided games in which there is no *offside rule* (see page 19). As players

The Discovery Method

One of the most effective ways of teaching children a skill is to use the *discovery method*—where they discover the answer for themselves. Here's how it works: you give players a demonstration of the technique you want them to learn. For example, if you wanted to teach them how to head the ball properly, instead of saying, "This is the part of the head you should use to head the ball," you say, "Watch this. You tell me which part of the player's head is being used to head the ball." Let your players tell you what is going on with the drill; let them explain it to you.

learn the game, you can gradually add end lines and sidelines. At that point you will have to determine how the ball comes back into play when it goes out of bounds. The standard rules of soccer call for *throw-ins*, *goal kicks*, and *corner kicks* (all discussed in this chapter) to cover all of the out-of-bounds possibilities, but these can be altered or simplified as you see fit. Each league will have its own rules as well. If the kids are young (under 11) and are playing 11-on-11 on a full field—which is not a good idea in my opinion—then sometimes an easier corner kick might be allowed from the junction of the end line and the *penalty area* (the rectangular area immediately in front of the goal) rather than the actual corner. Again, the league rules will dictate during games.

In general, I think coaches of young players should feel free to incorporate their own rules. Official rules are for referees and administrators. Coaches should just get the game going and then make little adjustments to make it a fun game. I don't take the results of youngsters' games too seriously. I am more concerned with a smooth game and the kids having fun than with teaching and adhering to specific rules. Time-outs are another example. Time-outs tend to be for coaches, so I am not greatly in favor of them. Time-outs stop the kids from thinking for themselves. The game should be the teacher, not the coach. Once the kids are involved with city and state leagues, all the rules will be laid down, but for young players, especially those under 10, I always say play until just before they are tired.

This book is about helping and encouraging a coach who wants to get a feeling for my philosophy in running a kid's team. I truly believe this world is far too full of rules. Let the kids play at practice, and when it comes to games I am sure there will be referees. When we had the Under-10s and the Under-12s originally playing their six-on-six soccer in the Upper Valley area of Hanover, New Hampshire, we purposely said that there would be no refs and no offside—just a parent encourager who made sure there were no bad fouls (pushing, an intentional trip, or intentionally touching the ball with your hands are all bad fouls) and the provision that when a sub wanted to come on, another player would have to come off. That was about it. Let the kids get on with the game. It is amazing how it will sort itself out. As a child, we never had an adult even supervising our soccer until I was 10 years old, and by then I had been playing steadily on the playground and in the park since the age of 6.

All that being said, I will offer the basics of soccer.

The Field

Officially speaking, a soccer field is a rectangle between 100 and 130 yards in length and between 50 and 100 yards in width. Dimensions of 100 yards by 70 yards are standard for a full-sized field. The field diagram in the appendix details the features of a regulation soccer field.

At each end of the field—along the goal line or end line—is a *goal*, which is 24 feet long and 8 feet high. The goal is indicated by goal posts and sometimes includes a net. Immediately in front of each goal is the *penalty area*. This 44-yard by 18-yard rectangle is the only area on the field where the goalkeeper may use his or her hands.

There are 11 players on each team: the goalkeeper and varying numbers of defenders, midfielders, and forwards. At the kickoff signaling the start of the half or the scoring of a goal, the goalie stands in front of her goal, and the defenders are spread across the field immediately in front of her. The midfielders line up midway between the centerline and the penalty area, and the forwards, or strikers, line up near the centerline. These positions are discussed in chapter 4.

Length of Game

A full-length game contains two 45-minute halves, with a short halftime intermission of 5–10 minutes. Youth games are shorter, with league rules setting the times for each age group.

Kickoff

A *kickoff* is used to begin play at the start of the game, after a goal, and after halftime. The ball is placed in the center circle of the field (see the field diagram in the appendix). The kicker is required to send the ball from the center circle into the opposing half of the field, and no player from the opposing side can be within 10 yards of the ball at the kickoff. All players must also remain in their half of the field until the ball is in play—which means it must travel the distance of its own circumference, or one rotation. The kicker may not touch the ball again until it is played by another player. Usually the team kicking off chooses to retain possession of the ball, with the first kicker tapping it to a teammate, but sometimes the kicker will send the ball deep into the opposite half.

A coin toss determines which team decides to kick off at the beginning of the game. At the start of the second half, teams switch goals, and the kickoff is made by the team that didn't kick off at the start of the game. Kickoffs also occur after a score—with the scored-upon team taking the kickoff.

Moving the Ball

Players can move the ball up the field by kicking and passing it or by using any other part of the body excluding the hands or arms. Except during a throw-in, which occurs after the ball is played out of bounds along the side-line (see below), only the goalie can pick up the ball with his or her hands. If a player accidentally touches the ball with his arm or hand, play continues. If the referee believes the touch was intentional, she'll stop play and call a foul.

Scoring

A goal is scored when the ball passes fully into the goal without being propelled by the hand or arm of an attacking player. In other words, get the ball in the net. One goal is worth one point.

The Goalkeeper

The goalkeeper defends the goal. Goalies are the only players who may use their hands to catch or propel the ball, as long as they remain within their own penalty area. However, when the ball is deliberately passed back by a member of her own team, the goalie must play the ball as if she were an outfield player. Since she is privileged to use her hands, the goalie must wear a different-colored shirt that distinguishes her from the rest of the team.

Out of Bounds

Action on the soccer field stops when the ball goes *out of bounds*, that is, travels outside the lines marking the playing field. The ball may be put back in play in one of three ways. A throw-in occurs if the ball goes over the side-lines; if it goes over the end line, then it's either a goal kick or corner kick.

- **Throw-in.** When one team causes the ball to go out of bounds by completely crossing a sideline (sometimes called a *touchline*), a *throw-in* is taken. Any player from the opposing team throws the ball back in play from the sideline with two hands on the ball. The ball must be thrown from behind and over the head, and both feet must remain on the ground throughout the throw. The player throwing in cannot play the ball until it has been touched by another player. (See the section on Throw-ins in chapter 4.)

- **Goal kick.** When the attacking team causes the ball to go out of bounds by completely crossing the goal line (the end line of the field excluding the goal itself), a *goal kick* is taken. Any member of the defending team kicks the ball back into play from anywhere inside the goal area. The kicker cannot play the ball again until it has been touched by another player. The attacking team must stay outside the penalty area during the kick, and the ball is not in play until it travels beyond the penalty area. A goal cannot be scored directly off a goal kick.

- **Corner kick.** When the defending team causes the ball to go out of bounds across the goal line, a *corner kick* is taken. Any member of the attacking team kicks the ball back into play from the corner area closest to where it went out of bounds. The kicker cannot play the ball again until it has been touched by another player. The defending team must stay at least 10 yards from the ball until it is in play. A goal can be scored directly off a corner kick.

Offside

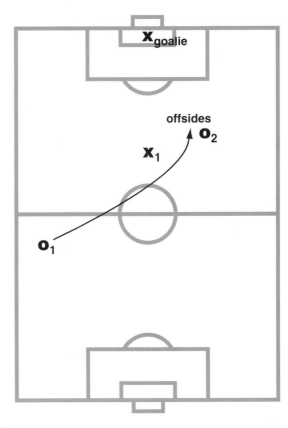

Player O_2, between the goalie and defender X_1, is offside.

The offside rule is designed to prevent flagrant goal-hanging by the attacking team. A player is offside when there is only one defensive player (including the goalie) between him and the goal. In order to be onside, the attacking player must be even with—or closer to—his own goal than two defensive players, including the goalie. In advanced level soccer it can often be a controversial call as to exactly when offside occurs. For young soccer players I prefer to keep it very simple and straightforward and only call the most obvious goal-hanging cases. When an offside violation is called, the attacking team loses possession, and an indirect free kick (see page 20) is taken by any member of the defending team from the spot where the violation occurred. I would not incorporate offside rules until kids start playing 11-on-11 on a full-size field.

Tie Scores

Soccer games can end in ties. Unless the league rule states otherwise, a tie will stand as a shared game.

Get into Their World

We were in the second day of the 112-team Dartmouth Cup, and Steve Swanson, the Dartmouth Women's Coach, and I were happily walking around the six-on-six tournament for kids under 10 years of age. It was going great, with shouts of excitement, but just as Steve and I were patting ourselves on the back for giving the kids a great weekend, an irate parent-coach stormed forward demanding whether we were responsible for this "mockery of soccer." We were, to put it mildly, taken aback and inquired about his complaint.

"Look at this," he raged, as he pointed out to the field. "There are balls flying from one field onto the other, and the kids don't know which ball to play."

I surveyed the field. Yes, there were four games going on adjacent to one another. We had quartered a full-sized Dartmouth field, and there were four six-on-six games going on. I then looked at the kids and responded, "But look at their faces. Every player is having a great time. Sure the balls are coming on and off various fields, but the kids are so into their own game that they don't even notice." I went on to point out that this wasn't meant to be the World Cup but was about youngsters having fun at a game. The kids were in their own little World Cup and were apparently having a great time, yet here was a parent-coach getting upset about adult concerns.

Sometimes we, as adults, forget about playing for the sake of playing. I can remember as a youngster playing "Cops and Robbers." We were totally involved in our own dramatic world. It is the same for all young kids. Don't take this romantic phase away from them. Try to come down to their level and make it seem like a World Cup. They will easily catch on. It is you, the parent, who has to get into their world a little.

Substitution

League rules dictate. In some leagues, substitutes may come onto the field only after the referee permits the change; other leagues allow running subs to come onto the field on the fly, when teammates leave the field, as in ice hockey.

Fouls

Free kicks

When a player commits a serious offense, the opposing team is awarded a *direct free kick*. This is a free kick from which a goal can be scored straight away—without any intervening play. Such offenses include deliberately kicking, tripping, striking, or holding an opponent. If any player handles the ball, or if the goalie handles the ball outside her own penalty area, a direct free kick is also awarded. (See the referee signals diagram in the appendix.)

An *indirect free kick* cannot result in a goal unless the ball is touched by someone else after the kicker and before it goes into the goal. An indirect kick is awarded for a less serious offense, including playing in a dangerous manner, deliberately obstructing an opponent when not playing the ball, unsportsmanlike conduct, and too many players on the field.

A free kick, whether direct or indirect, is taken from the spot where the violation occurred by any member of the fouled team. The opposing team must stay at least 10 yards away from the ball until it is put into play (unless they are guarding the goal between their own goalposts). If the kick is being taken from inside the penalty area, the opposing team must remain outside it.

Penalty kick

If a defending player commits a violation within his own penalty area that warrants a direct free kick, a penalty kick is awarded. The kick is taken from the penalty spot, which is 12 yards from the goal, unless league rules state otherwise. The goalie can move sideways but not forward in the goal until the kick is taken, and all players apart from the kicker and the goalie must stay outside the penalty area and 10 yards from the ball. An indirect free kick awarded within the penalty area is taken as a regular indirect free kick.

Modified Field Size and Rules

Players under the age of eight should ideally play four-on-four games of soc-cer on a field 40 yards by 35 yards, with goals that are 6 yards wide by 6 feet high. There should be no offside rules, just throw-ins, corner kicks, and goal kicks.

In my experience, kids between the ages of 8 and 12 do best in seven-on-seven games played on half a full-sized field (50 by 70 yards) with no off-side rules, just throw-ins, corner kicks, and goal kicks. The size of the goal is not overly important, but I would say a 10-yard goal area would suffice, with a goal 7 yards wide and 7 feet high.

The Importance of Small-Sided Games

When I was back in Scotland, I coached soccer for the little two-teacher school that my own children attended in Maryculter, a rural area where we were living. The entire school had only 24 kids, from grades 1 through 7. All of the schools in this area of Aberdeenshire were about the same size, and all had a soc-cer league going. When I started coaching the Maryculter Eagles, the league played 11-on-11 games. My first impression was that the kids were not really involved in the games. They weren't having as much fun as they should, so I proposed that the format be changed to seven players a side, with no offside rules and running subs. I still feel that was one of the most positive things I did for all the little soccer players in that country area. It helped develop the better players and allowed the less-skilled ones to also have far more ball touches. We all had a great time.

Once the players move into 11-on-11 play on a full-sized field (70 by 100 yards), the normal (adult) rules of soccer would take effect, and offside would be introduced.

A full-size field is usually recognized as 120 by 75 yards (see field diagram in the appendix), although fields can be bigger. For youngsters U-12, I would advise a field 100 by 70 yards. To be honest, I believe that 115 by 75 yards is an ideal size for any age right up to professionals. In the recent World Cups, FIFA has recommended 115 by 75 yards.

CHAPTER 3

Setting Up the Season

One of the most daunting challenges a new coach faces is how to organize all the facets of a season: how many practices to have in a week, where to get uniforms, who is responsible for the equipment, how to contact everyone if practice is canceled—the list of details goes on and on. The best defense against administrative quicksand is a good offense: plan your season ahead of time. The more energy you can devote to coaching, the better.

Get Some Help

Take Advantage of Parent Volunteers

Is there a parent who seems enthusiastic and eager to help? Enlist him or her to be the team manager—the person who organizes transportation to away games, the phone tree for bad weather or canceled practices, and the team dinners and meetings. This is a big job, and divesting yourself of these responsibilities will make you a much happier—and more effective—coach.

Find an Assistant

If possible, find a college or high school player to help assist you during practices and games. Most high school and college players will have mastered the techniques and game skills that you might not have polished (or even know). Coaching assistants are great, not only because they can demonstrate drills and plays and can serve as terrific role models for your players, but also because you can play off of them personality wise. Use your assistant to get your team interested and involved in the practice. A good assistant can be an invaluable asset to a youth team, and you will be grateful for the physical, and moral, support.

Jobs for the Team Manager

1. **Phone tree.** It is important to have a good communication system so that 25 soccer players aren't calling you every time it rains. One of the most important jobs the team manager has is to set up a phone-tree calling protocol for bad weather, canceled games or practices, or other messages for players or parents. The way the phone tree operates is that you call the team manager with whatever message you want to convey; the manager relays the message to several parent volunteers (probably two to four parents, or a few more if you have a large team); and these parents phone the rest of the team. This is a quick and convenient way to contact all your players, and each caller needs to make only a few phone calls.

2. **Travel plans.** When your team has an away game, it is a good idea to have a central meeting place to start the trip so that everyone gets off at the same time and in the same direction. The manager is responsible for arranging car pools and for distributing maps and travel instructions.

3. **Uniforms.** Many youth league players come to their first few practices without the proper equipment. One way to avoid this is to have the team manager arrange a sign-up night at the local sports store so that the kids are signed up for the team and outfitted at the same time. Most sports stores will give significant discounts to team purchases. If your soccer league provides uniforms for the players, the manager can be in charge of distributing the uniforms and then rounding them up at the end of the season.

4. **Team dinners, fund-raisers, and other social events.** Most youth league teams need to raise money for one thing or another, and any team worth its stuff will have at least one team dinner during the season. These events are great for fostering team spirit and can be arranged by the team manager, who should take advantage of the talents and expertise of the other parents on the team as well.

A good assistant, in this instance my son Tommy, can be an invaluable asset.

Set the Ground Rules with Your Assistant

Make sure that you explain your philosophy and expectations for behavior during the season, not only to your players and their parents, but to your assistant as well. You don't want to be out on the field with an assistant who doesn't share your philosophy of good sportsmanship, patience, or keeping things fun, and you need to make this clear before the season starts.

Meet the Parents

It is important to sit down with parents to outline your coaching philosophy and expectations for the season *before it starts*. At the same time, parents can determine what the guidelines for the season will be—for them and their children. Everyone should agree at the beginning, before a ball is kicked, that the kids are there to learn, to play in the spirit of the game, to observe the rules, and to act properly. Once the games start, things sometimes change—parents who were seemingly very understanding, quiet, and helpful at the beginning are often the ones who are yelling at the referees and causing problems. You will need to address what problems may arise and then collectively set some guidelines—but let parents come up with the rules for their behavior, with some direction from you.

Issues such as playing time and proper game etiquette for everyone—parents, players, and you, the coach—should be discussed and agreed upon before the meeting is over. The points I would want to stress with parents: let's have fun; this is for the kids, not the parents; and let's see how we can draw up some plans to make sure that you, the parents, and I, the coach, can make this happen. I never tell people anything, and it's important in this meeting not to be a know-it-all coach. I always try to lead parents into a good situation, because if you try to dictate, people put up barriers. From my experience, most parents will see logic at a preseason meeting. That is when you make the rules together. Once the season is underway, and the games are being played, it is sometimes too late.

Guidelines you might suggest to parents include
- positive encouragement
- coaches coach and spectators spectate
- politeness
- treating the referees with respect
- no yelling at the kids and especially no yelling of negative comments

But first, let the parents have the opportunity to suggest these guidelines. If the parents come up with the charter, then their only option is to abide by it. You should moderate and guide the discussion, but be sure to let the parents themselves agree on what the guidelines should be—they will have a vested interest in adhering to such guidelines and will also feel they had a voice in determining the tone of the season.

Agreeing on guidelines beforehand won't guarantee that Jimmy's dad will refrain from second-guessing every decision you make on the field, but both you and he will know the issue was raised, discussed, and addressed. Here are some topics to cover during the parents meeting:

- Expectations they have for the season
- Expectations you have for the season
- Establishing playing time, substitution policy, does everyone play? Explain to parents how this will work and elicit their feedback
- Practice and game punctuality
- Etiquette on and off the field for players, coaches, and parents
- Based on the parent guidelines, how to address problems that arise for anyone—including you

Establish Your Policies

Practice Schedule

Not only do you need to decide how many practices you should have per week (two a week plus a game is a general standard), but you also need to determine where your usual practice field will be, what time you will hold practice, and what you will do in the event of bad weather. While it is easy to call off practice because of bad weather, canceling should always be a last resort. The fickleness of Mother Nature means that, as often as not, the weather won't be perfect every time you want to practice—or play a game. Learning to play in less than ideal conditions is just part of the sport. Be creative and find a way to hold some kind of practice in every kind of weather.

Lateness and Missed Practices

Because most of your players are at the mercy of their parents' schedules, you will need to be somewhat flexible in how you deal with tardiness and missed practices. At the same time, however, players who are not on time or don't make it to practice should recognize that this is not okay. The best way to deal with occasional lateness is to create a light forfeit rather than a punishment for lateness, such as having that player collect the equipment at the end of practice. This way, your players recognize that you don't approve of their tardiness, but you don't have to make a big issue of it. Chronic lateness or missed practices should certainly be addressed by talking to the parent. It is important for both parents and players to know that once players have made commitments to a team, they are obliged to come to all the practices they can.

Uniforms and Equipment

Whether your league pays for your uniforms or not, you will most likely be responsible for obtaining them for your team members. The best and most practical uniforms for youth players are a T-shirt and shorts. Ideally, players should have both practice and game T-shirts: the kids will look like a team, and looking like a team helps them play more like a team as well.

Equipment needs for soccer are mercifully minimal. As a coach, you'll need small, flat plastic cones that are ideal for lining out a field; long, conical plastic cones; pinnies (lightweight vests) in two colors; a ball pump; balls; and soccer nets. Try to have all of your players bring their own balls to practice so that everyone has a ball to use. You should always bring a pump so that the balls are properly inflated. You can purchase collapsible goals for practice, but try to make sure they are netted goals. There is nothing more exciting for a young player than to kick a ball into the goal and have it caught in the net. Conversely, there's nothing more frustrating for a kid than to kick a great goal and then have to run thirty yards to retrieve the ball.

Equipment requirements for soccer are mercifully minimal. If you can, have your players bring their own balls to practice.

For footwear, I always prefer that players wear cleats, which provide better grip than sneakers. Although sneakers can serve the purpose when the ground is hard, when the ground is wet they give no traction and put the player at a disadvantage. The molded cleat is the best type for younger players. I would advise detachable studs only for advanced players on a wet field.

Players 7 years old and younger should really be playing with a #3 size ball; use #4 for 12 years and under and #5 for over 12. The general rule is that the younger the player, the smaller the foot, which means smaller balls for smaller feet.

Although some young players will insist to their parents they need knee pads to play soccer properly, I've found that knee pads restrict move-

Equipment Checklist

- small, flat plastic cones to mark field
- long, conical plastic cones to mark goals, drills
- pinnies (vests) in two colors
- two or three soccer balls, more if possible
- ball pump
- collapsible or permanent goals with nets, if possible
- first-aid kit and ice pack
- whistle
- clipboard
- team roster

ment and serve no great purpose for a field player. I do, however, recommend knee pads for goalkeepers.

Questions and Answers

Q. No one has volunteered to be the team manager for my team, and I'm feeling completely overwhelmed. What do I do?

A. You really can't do a good coaching job if you're spending your time doing all the administrative work, too. Getting overwhelmed will take the fun out of the job for you. The best advice is not to get yourself into this position—contact every parent on the team if you have to in order to solicit help of some kind. You shouldn't have to do everything, and you will need to make that clear to parents if no one offers to lend a hand.

Q. Where do I find out the details of practice and game scheduling? Do I have to call the school or recreation department to arrange field time, call coaches to set up games? Is this something I have to take care of myself, or does the league do it, or what?

A. Most leagues set up a schedule of games and fields for practice. It's a good idea to check in with your recreation department or league administrator to confirm the schedule, especially for games. Before playing another team, you might want to call the other coach to make sure that his or her schedule matches yours regarding time and place. Most leagues will supply the names and phone numbers of other coaches. If the league does not schedule field times for practices, have your team manager locate a convenient field available at the times you want to hold practices.

No Ball, No Shoes, No Field, No Coach

When I was coaching the Highlanders Football Club in Zimbabwe, I really loved the basic enthusiasm of the country for soccer. All over the city of Bulawayo on bits of waste ground there were little games of soccer going on. There wasn't an adult in sight, and the field was usually hard, red, uneven, African hardpan without a single blade of grass. There were no goals, just a couple of rocks to signify a goal. There was seldom a proper ball but instead a plastic bag stuffed with paper or rags. The players also did not have soccer shoes and in most cases played in bare feet. At first glance it would seem that it would be difficult to play and produce proper soccer players, but the opposite is the case: Africa produces some of the best technical players in the world. What these players all seemed to have was a love for playing the game, and because the game is their teacher, they develop wonderful imaginative minds to go with their natural skills. I recall Methembe Ndlovu, who came to the United States to play for me at Dartmouth from Highlanders FC, telling me that he didn't get his first pair of real soccer shoes until he was 16.

In some ways we were a little the same when I was growing up in Scotland. Perhaps one boy on the street would have a real soccer ball, but most of the games were played on a school playground with a tennis ball. A tennis ball then cost sixpence, and the slang for a sixpence in those days was a "tanner." Hence Scotland was famed through that era for producing players who had great skills and were dubbed "Tanner Ba'" players.

Q. Most of the parents I've talked to don't have time to have a "parents-only" meeting with me. Do I call each one individually, write a letter, or what? How important is it to meet with them before the season?

A. Meet with those who can come to discuss the season. For those who can't make it, write up your expectations and rules, and put out a letter to them. If they disagree with what you've written, they can get in touch with you to talk about it. It's a good idea to give parents a choice of meeting with you, regardless of how many can come, to keep the lines of communication open.

Q. My son's entire grade signed up to play soccer, and now I'm the coach of 50 second-graders with only one assistant. What do I do?

A. This is a pleasant problem, because you never want to turn kids away. Two people can handle a large group of kids with some careful planning. Young players will spend much of their time on the very basic skills, and the drills for these are all done as a group, anyway. It's important that each child brings a ball to practice so that everyone can practice the skills at the same time. You will need to be organized in advance for the games at the end of the practice so that it isn't bedlam as you divide up your players. Try and enlist some parent assistants. Take advantage of parents who are watching the practice—with your players at such a young age, many parents will be on the sidelines. They don't need to know anything about the sport at this age and skill level, so encourage them to help by monitoring groups for squabbles or other complications.

Sample Preseason Letter to Parents

Dear Parents:

Another soccer season is upon us. I'm excited about our team and hope your kids are, too.

My primary goal for the season is for everyone to have fun and improve their soccer skills. My basic philosophy is to foster a positive, supportive atmosphere so that every player has a great experience. Regardless of ability, every member of the team deserves to be treated with encouragement. Players should respect each other on and off the field and should learn both to win and lose well. I look to you to help reinforce these important concepts: when you come to games and practices, please limit your interaction with your children to positive encouragement from a distance. During games, please sit on the other side of the field from our team, and please treat the referees with the respect they deserve. We are our children's most important role models. I will set as good an example as I possibly can, and I would greatly appreciate your help by doing the same.

Games: Please make every effort to have your child at our games 30 minutes before the scheduled start. If you know that getting your child to a game will be difficult, we can carpool. If your child cannot make it to a game, please let me know in advance. If your child misses practice the week before the game without a good reason, he or she might not play in the game. Please know that I have this policy so that participation in the games is fair for everyone.

Cancellation: Unless you hear otherwise, we will always have practice or games. In the case of cancellation, kids will be notified either at school or by means of the enclosed phone tree.

Must Bring: Please make sure that your child has a water bottle, soccer ball, sneakers (or cleats), shin guards, shorts, and either a T-shirt for practice or the game shirt for a game. Balls and water bottles should be labeled.

We're looking forward to a great season of soccer. If you have questions or concerns, please feel free to contact me.

Thanks,
The Coach
403 Lincoln Avenue
555-4007
coach@soccer.com

Q. I have two volunteer assistants who both have had some experience coaching. Unfortunately, they both have very different ideas about what we should do during practice. What's the best way to incorporate their ideas?

A. Remember that you are the coach here, and you will set both the agenda and the tone for practice. They have to interpret your views, since you are the head of the team. You can also split up the practice and let them take charge of certain sections, such as the warm-up or the ball-handling section, but they must always be doing something you accept or condone or are comfortable with.

Q. How long should my practices be?

A. I believe that age should dictate the length of practice. For kids under 8, practices should be no longer than 75 minutes. For kids 8 to 12, practices shouldn't go over 90 minutes, and even for players over 12, I rarely go over 90 minutes. Two hours is always the absolute maximum for any practice.

CHAPTER 4

Essential Skills— and How to Teach Them

The Fundamentals

Good soccer players make the game look effortless: they move down the field, barely touching the ball, weaving among defenders like they are threading a needle, and then make a perfect shot to score. But soccer is a game where mastering such ball-handling skills doesn't come easily or quickly. In fact, even world-class players constantly practice the basic, but crucial, fundamentals of dribbling, passing and receiving, heading, shooting, and defending to hone and perfect their game. Your job as coach is to help your players learn the fundamentals to give them a solid foundation of skills that they can practice through a lifetime in the sport.

How to Use My Drills and Games

For the most part I have not classified my drills and games according to any scale of difficulty or age appropriateness. Most of the drills and games start out slowly, and you will soon feel your way forward. What the children learn from a specific drill will depend on their level of development. The majority of these games work equally well for the youngest beginners on up to the older, more experienced players. The only really advanced drills are the three-on-one (such as Piggy in the Middle, game 32), Four-on-Two Keep Away (game 33), Two-Zone Soccer (game 55), and Three-Zone Soccer (game 56)(see chapter 9).

     The thinking is the key behind this book, not the actual drills. Competition is what's important for the kids, and even more essential is how they handle that competition. Get to know your group of kids and use your judgment about what you think will work for your group.

Advice on Teaching Fundamentals

The most effective way to teach the fundamental principles of any skill is to briefly demonstrate the skill; then let your players try it on their own (see the Discovery Method sidebar on page 16). After players have had a chance to try the skill, bring them in around you again and demonstrate one more time, highlighting the part of the skill that they may not be getting. You will most likely find that 80 percent will pick up the basics of proper technique during the first demonstration, and the other 20 percent will pick it up during the second demonstration. The key is to keep the demonstrations focused on small increments—don't try to show the entire skill in one demonstration. Rather, have your players work on one part of the skill at a time. After you have demonstrated the skill a second time, let them try it again. Then bring your players in around you and ask them questions about their technique, such as, "What part of your foot do you use to kick the ball? Where is the ball when you do a spin?" After they have answered your questions, send them out onto the field once again and have them respond to your commands while practicing the skill.

Although you should always encourage kids to kick with both feet and to work on getting comfortable with either foot, when I introduce a skill, I always have players use their stronger foot. Once they have a clear picture of how to perform the skill, they can then start using their weaker foot.

Summary of introducing a new soccer skill:

- demonstration
- let players try
- demonstration
- let players try
- questions and answers
- have players respond to commands while practicing the skill

Minor Injuries? Think RICE

Bumps and bruises are a part of soccer. If your player's injury needs more attention than the following, be sure to contact your local emergency room or physician. For minor sprains and strains, however, the RICE method will help a minor soft tissue injury heal faster.

- **Relative Rest.** Avoid activities that exacerbate the injury, but continue to move the injured area gently. Early gentle movement promotes healing.

- **Ice.** Apply ice to the affected area for 20 minutes; then leave it off for at least an hour. Do not use ice if you have circulatory problems.

- **Compression.** Compression creates a pressure gradient that reduces swelling and promotes healing. An elastic bandage provides a moderate amount of pressure that will help discourage swelling.

- **Elevation.** Elevation is especially effective when used in conjunction with compression. Elevation provides a pressure gradient: the higher the injured body part is raised, the more fluid is pulled away from the injury site via gravity. Elevate the injury as high above the heart as comfortable. Continue to elevate intermittently until swelling is gone.

Dribbling

Learning to move with the ball is perhaps the most important primary skill in soccer. Not only do players have to learn the proper technique for moving the ball on the field, they also have to learn to keep their heads up, look around the field, and assess what is happening in the game. The better players are at moving with the ball, the more confident they will become. One of the best aspects of dribbling is that it can be practiced virtually anywhere there is a flat surface with room to move, and players can do it on their own.

Learning to move comfortably with the ball is perhaps the game's most important skill.

The Principles

There are four key concepts to dribbling:

- **Foot position.** The player dribbles the ball by initiating contact with the top of her foot at about the lower part of the laces. Many times a beginning player will try to run with ball on the inside of her foot, with the foot turned out. Instead, a player should run with her foot straight ahead, with the ball in front of her. As she touches the ball, her foot should turn slightly inward, which helps control the ball.

- **Ball position.** The ball should be approximately a yard or so in front of the player, within playing distance but not right underneath the feet. The biggest mistake young players make in dribbling is trying to keep the ball too close to their bodies.

- **Turning/changing direction.** Players need to be able to change direction quickly and efficiently. *Turning* is stopping the ball's movement by putting one foot on top of the ball to stop it and then pivoting over and around the ball in a variety of directions, including turning to the outside. A *step-over turn* is achieved when the player steps over the ball and then immediately places his foot on top of the ball and moves it in a different direction.

One big mistake beginners make is trying to run with the ball on the inside of their feet. Remind players to use the top of their feet, not the instep, to move the ball forward.

Have your players keep the ball a yard or so in front of them, within playing distance but not right underneath the feet.

- **Playing both feet.** It is important to learn to move the ball comfortably with both feet. Players have to be able to take the ball from one foot and put it on to the other foot quickly when they are defending the ball from opponents.

To turn, the player stops the ball's movement by putting one foot on top, as shown, and then pivots over and around the ball.

How to Teach Dribbling

The best way to become comfortable dribbling the ball is to play games that keep your players interested and having fun while practicing a skill in a competitive environment.

Dribbling Skills

- heads-up dribbling
- foot position
- ball position
- turning/changing direction
- playing both feet
- a sense of space and keeping the field covered

Dribbling Drills and Games

The following drills and games are described in detail in chapter 9.

One of the games I use to help kids work on their dribbling skills is called Spaceman (see game 14 on page 100). The game is designed to keep players moving the ball, but it also requires them to think, keep their heads up while they're dribbling, and gain a sense of space on the field. The key to teaching dribbling, like other fundamentals, is to let the game do the work—give the kids the basic instructions for the game, and let them go. They'll catch on very quickly to what they need to do.

Create a large square space on the field, approximately 30 yards by 30 yards. Have your players dribble around the square. Tell them that they are spacemen and that they need to fill up the space in the square while they dribble. Ask them questions throughout the drill such as, "Are you watching your space?" and "Where are the holes?" This will help them keep their heads up and be aware of where the other players are. When you shout, "Stop," everyone freezes. Your players should be evenly spaced within the square. If they are well distributed, then you have to pay the forfeit, such as ten push-ups or something they come up with. If players are concentrated in some areas, and large patches of the square are bare, they pay a forfeit.

Players will learn that when one kid moves out of a space, someone else must move into that space. And that, really, is one of the fundamentals of the game of soccer: continuous movement with everybody's eyes up, concentrating on filling the space.

Passing and Receiving

Learning to pass and receive the ball properly is a key fundamental for soccer success. Passing requires not only good foot technique but also an ability to read and assess other players—it is the foundation for team play.

Passing

There are three main principles to good passing: direction, pace, and proper technique. The pace of the pass is equally as important as the direction of the pass; if a ball is passed too hard or soft, it is difficult for young players to

Be Alert to Health Problems

There's nothing more frightening for a parent—or coach—than to see a child in distress and not know what to do. Breathing problems, including exercise-induced asthma, are more prevalent in children than ever before. Make sure that you talk to parents about how important it is for you to be aware of any pre-existing physical condition that any of your players may have. In addition, parents need to give you as much information as possible about what to do if their child is in distress, and who to contact if problems occur. Forewarned is forearmed.

Most recreational leagues and schools will have health questionnaires and liability releases. If the league or school doesn't take care of this, getting parents to complete a brief questionnaire should alert you to potential major health issues. Having the league director review the questionnaire before you send it to parents could help make sure you ask all the *necessary* questions.

To keep their feet from digging into the field, get your players to think of their passing leg as a putter.

receive it properly or effectively. The two most basic passes are the *inside-foot pass* and the *outside-foot pass*, although players can pass with many other different surfaces of the body.

How to Teach Passing

When passing to another player, the passer moves the ball with the inside (or outside) of her foot, with the toe up, ankle locked, and foot firm. The player then follows through with her foot, keeping the toe up and the foot firm. Her standing foot is placed alongside the ball.

A good way to describe proper pass technique is to compare the passer's foot to a putter. The biggest mistake most youngsters make when passing is to jam their foot into the ground as they pass. But if you tell your players to compare their passing foot to a putter, you can then ask them, "When a golfer makes a putt, does he putt and end up with a putter in the ground? No, he doesn't. He follows through to the target. It's the same when you're playing your pass. Follow through. Make your foot follow through and pass." Comparing what you want players to learn to something else they may be familiar with is a good way for them to visualize the proper position for the skill.

Setting up the pass properly with a *preparation touch* is as important as sending it off. A good way to explain the importance of setting up a pass properly is to tell your players that they are really doing two passes: when they receive the ball, the first pass is a small pass to themselves to set up the ball, and the next pass is to their teammate. That little pass allows the player to get his head up and see the target. At the same time, it helps move the

To help your players get used to heads-up passing and receiving, pair them up and have them work at receiving the ball in front of them with one touch of the foot and passing it back with the second touch.

Passing and Receiving Skills

- direction
- pace
- proper technique
- inside-foot pass and out-side-foot pass
- preparation touch
- quick foot movement
- heads-up passing

Passing and Receiving Drills and Games

The following drills and games are described in detail in chapter 9.

ball far enough in front of the player so he can still see the ball and do the second pass to the receiver. This is called the preparation touch because the player touches the ball once to set it up and then passes it on to another receiver.

Receiving

The most important aspect of receiving the ball effectively is for the player to capture the ball with one touch and then move her feet quickly to get in behind the ball again to take control and either dribble or pass. This can often be a problem for many young players, who don't move their feet quickly enough and end up stabbing at the ball rather than controlling it. In a good pass reception, both the foot and the head come up. If a player can arrest the ball with one touch, her head comes up immediately after reception, and she is already surveying the field and making decisions. If a player needs to take another touch to set the ball up, then her head goes down again. The more times players look down, the less time they have to observe and plan. Your goal is to teach your players "heads-up soccer."

A good way to help your players get used to heads-up passing and receiving is to divide them into pairs and have them work on receiving the ball in front of them with one touch of the foot and passing it back with the second touch. When your players are making an inside-of-the-foot pass, it's important for the standing foot to be placed alongside the ball, so that they come in behind the ball, not across the ball.

Ball Control

Kids should begin working on their *ball control*, often referred to as touch or juggling, right from the beginning. Good control allows players to get their heads up and make decisions. When receiving a pass, if a player is able to set up the ball with her first touch, she can then get her head up immediately. Every body surface, except the hands and arms, is important in controlling a soccer ball. Just look at any top player: no matter how the ball comes to him, he will tame it. In a game of soccer the ball does not always come along the ground. It often is in the air or is bouncing, so the player must be comfortable making contact with the ball while it is in the air.

The best way to develop a touch and feel for the ball is *juggling*: keeping the ball in the air with the feet or other body surfaces except for the hands and arms. But how does a youngster begin to get a feel for the ball? It is diffi-

cult to just start juggling the ball, or playing "Keepy Up," as we used to call it in Scotland. When we were kids, Keepy Up was always a standard by which we judged ourselves. We worked hard to see how many times we could juggle the ball without it touching the ground. For a young player it can be a very short session, since the ball is always on the ground. (See Keepy Up on page 109 of chapter 9.)

A good way to introduce juggling or Keepy Up is to start with what I call one touch/one bounce. The player starts by holding the ball. She drops it and touches it with her instep (where the laces of the shoe are), lets it bounce on the ground, touches it again with the instep, lets it bounce on the ground, and keeps the sequence going. Once your players can handle

"Keepy Up" is a great way to practice ball-handling skills.

twenty consecutive sequences of one touch/one bounce, start a game of two touch/one bounce, using alternate feet. When that has been mastered, take them onto the Keepy-Up Ladder. This is simply the sequence when the player starts with one touch/one bounce, goes to two touches/one bounce, on to three touches/one bounce, and keeps adding on a touch until she hits 10 touches. If she doesn't make it to 10 touches before missing, she just goes back to the first step on the ladder and starts climbing up again. The coach can then ask, "How high up the ladder did you get?" or "Can you beat last week's record?"

What's great about this drill is that all the kids can do it at their own level. Some can be at one touch/one bounce, some at two touches and a bounce, and some further up the ladder. Allowing the players to put a bounce in helps them control the ball, so they can be successful right from the start. As their confidence grows, you can introduce the thigh, chest, and head as alternative surfaces of control. Different parts of the foot, the inside or even the heel, can be introduced for the most exceptional players. This is also a great doggy bag exercise for your team and will promote confidence (see the Doggy Bag and Final Meeting section in chapter 5). As the players improve, they can begin doing the same exercises in pairs, juggling the ball back and forth between them, first with one touch/one bounce, then two touches, and then up the ladder. And with advanced kids in their teens, you can even take out the bounce.

When receiving a ball, *control* can also be called *trapping*, although I don't like the word because it sounds harsh to me. Controlling a bouncing ball should be smooth. Select the surface—head, chest, thigh—use a preparatory touch, and finish it off with the inside or outside of the foot. I like to begin with every player having a ball. Players just throw the ball a little ways into the air, use a body surface, say a thigh, to play the ball, and finish it off with the foot. As confidence grows, do the exercise in pairs. One player throws the ball to her partner, who selects the surface for the preparatory touch and controls the ball. As players really gain confidence, the one who throws the ball to her partner can then pressure the ball, so that the receiver must control the ball and move it out of reach of her opponent with the first touch.

Stress Individual Goals

When kids are learning to control the ball, it is important to stress that they should work toward individual goals. There will always be some players who excel at ball control, and some who don't. You need to be careful that the players who aren't as proficient don't get discouraged because they aren't as good at certain skills as some other players. Rather than challenging your players to excel by saying, "Who can beat the team record with this drill?" make the challenge an individual one. Make sure every player is working toward a personal, realistic goal so that they all feel they are improving—working to accomplish something that is achievable for them.

Shooting

Shooting the ball into the net is the glamour skill of soccer—it's the part of the game that everyone wants to do well. Shooting is also one of the most difficult skills to master for young players, because technique is so important.

The Principles

There are many different ways to shoot a ball—advanced players can even put a spin on it with the inside or the outside of the foot so that the shot "bends" around an obstacle toward the goal. However, the first and most important way to shoot that young players should learn is to strike the ball with the instep—the hard bone on the top of their foot—with their toe pointed and their ankle locked.

How to Teach Shooting

Striking the ball with the instep is possibly one of the hardest things for a kid to understand and accomplish well. One reason is that many young players aren't exactly sure what or where the instep is. Show your players where their insteps are and where the laces of their shoes are. Explain to them that if they hit the ball with something hard, such as their insteps, the ball will go much faster.

When striking the ball for a shot, the players' toe should be pointed and the ankle locked. Some people actually do this with no shoe on, striking the ball with their bare feet. This teaches players not to hit the ball with

To shoot correctly, the player strikes the ball with the instep, keeping the toe pointed and the ankle locked.

Shooting Skills

- striking the ball with the instep
- proper technique
- accuracy and control

Shooting Drills and Games

The following drills and games are described in detail in chapter 9.

the toe, since it hurts, although I don't recommend this method for young players. Quite often it's good to have your players sit down and point to their insteps, so that it's clear that they know what part of the foot you're talking about. Then have them just touch the ball with their foot in the proper position so they get a lot of little touches with the ball and the foot to get a feel for how they should be striking the ball. As they become more comfortable with the technique, they can stand up and progress on to small volleys, working on proper technique. It is always a good idea to start off slowly and gently, working on good form.

Without accuracy and control, shooting is just kicking the ball hard. Simple target games are the best way to help beginning players develop accurate shooting. For example, in the Target Shooting game (see game 37 on page 110), pairs of players stand about 25 yards apart and take turns shooting at a cone or ball midway between them. By keeping score of the "hits," you can add a competitive element and keep your players engaged in this simple but critical drill.

Heading

Soccer is the only sport where players hit the ball with their heads to pass, score, clear, or control the ball—thus *heading* is a vital part of the game. Heading can also be one of the most intimidating fundamentals for young players to learn, primarily because they are afraid they'll get hurt. The best way to minimize their concern is to emphasize proper technique and show them that the more aggressive they are with their heading, the better and more effective they will be.

The Principles

Heading has three main principles:

- Players should meet the ball forcefully, not wait for the ball to hit them.
- Players should meet the ball with their forehead, keeping their eyes open and their mouths closed.
- The power of heading should come from the body, not the legs.

How to Teach Heading

The most important points to emphasize when teaching kids to head the ball properly are for them to have their eyes wide open when they head the ball, and to hit the ball with their foreheads. The best way to begin is to just touch the ball onto their heads. Challenge them to keep their eyes open. Next, throw the ball up just a little bit and demonstrate doing little headers by yourself, just giving the ball a little touch. Have players try to throw a ball up gently and head it. Then ask them if they could head it twice in a row—give them a challenge, and they'll become so involved in the game that they forget to be intimidated.

When players gain a little confidence, discuss technique. Have them pair off, sitting facing each other, toes touching and knees bent. One partner throws the ball up and heads it to his partner. The partner catches the ball, throws it up in the air, and heads it back. Because they are sitting down, they can't use their legs—all the power has to come from their bodies, especially from their stomach and back muscles. Have players move farther and farther apart as they get more proficient.

Once they've done this, they go onto their knees and do the same drill. This can be difficult, since they need to be careful not to overbalance—they shouldn't fall forward on their hands. Have them move farther apart as they get the feel for the motion and the controlled body movement.

Finally, have players stand a shoulder width apart. One player throws the ball up in the air and heads it to her partner without overbalancing either forward or backward. Again, have the players gradually move farther apart until they are out of range.

Heading Skills

- meeting the ball forcefully
- meeting the ball with the forehead
- using the power of the body, not the legs
- accuracy

Heading Drills and Games

The following drills and games are described in detail in chapter 9.

- Glasgow Kisses 41
- Heading Ladder 42
- Standing Head Game 43
- Two-on-Two Heading 44
- Rommel's Desert War 45
- Heading Triangle 46
- Throw-Head-Catch (Team Handball) 47
- Head Tennis 48
- Heading Soccer 49

When heading, remember to use your forehead, keep your eyes open, and keep your mouth closed.

Seated heading drills are a great way to teach good form.

As your players practice these one-on-one heading drills, they'll begin to gain some accuracy through controlling their body movements slightly and subtly. Accuracy comes with practice.

Goalkeeping

Goalkeeping, or preventing the ball from entering the soccer goal, is a hugely important part of the game, requiring some different, specialized skills. Some youth league teams have players who play only goal, while others rotate their players in all positions. Whatever your league does, it's important to remember to include your goalie in as much of the general practice as possible, so that he learns solid overall soccer skills.

One good way to help your goalie hone her goalie-specific skills is to have a "Goalie Night" with all the goalies in the league. You and the other coaches can gather all of the young goalies and help them learn together such basics as catching the three shots and learning to fall. The goalies will learn much more by watching their peers than they would just practicing on their own.

Goalies have clothing and equipment that other players don't; they usually wear gloves and, often, padded shirts for extra protection. Many goalies wear knee pads or long pants, or both, when fields are hard or the weather is cold—these help prevent scrapes and bumps and will keep their legs warmer, since they're not running around as much as other players. Sometimes goalies wear longer, tighter-fitting underpants to prevent their thighs from getting grass burns.

The Principles

There are three types of shots to goal: high, mid, and low. Footwork is important in catching the ball, and each type of shot requires a different catching technique.

- High shots in the goalkeeper's range. The key to defending high shots on goal is for the goalie to have his thumbs in a good W position: thumbs together, palms up, and fingers spread. His head should be steady, with his eyes open, and movement should come from his feet. The goalie should move from behind the ball to deflect it or catch it before it goes in the goal.
- Mid shots in the goalkeeper's range. When balls come toward the goalie at her midsection, she should tuck her elbows in and have her hands in a good position to bring the ball in toward her body. Goalies should think of their hands and arms as strings, pulling the ball straight into their bodies, so that they absorb the ball. Again, the movement should come from the feet.
- Low shots in the goalkeeper's range. When a ball is low to the ground, the goalie should come out to the ball rather than wait to meet it. If it is a soft, slow shot, the goalie should get a leg behind him, keep his arms low

Below left. It's important for goalies to keep their heads steady and their eyes on the ball when deflecting or catching a ball in goal.

Below right. Good hand position is an essential component of goalkeeping. Note the W the goalie's hands make to deflect the shot.

Goalkeeping Skills

- proper technique for catching high shots
- proper technique for catching mid shots
- proper technique for catching low shots
- boxing and deflecting
- proper technique for falling
- outlet passes
- drop kicks and punts

Goalkeeping Drills and Games

The following drills and games are described in detail in chapter 9.

and ready, and scoop up the ball. If it is a hard, fast ball, the goalie should get down behind the ball and try to catch it, again absorbing the ball.

How to Teach Goalkeeping

Goalies must develop the skills of deflecting the ball, falling the proper way, making outlet passes, and kicking the ball into the offensive zone.

- **Boxing and deflecting shots.** The goalkeeper "boxes" a shot when she uses her fist to punch a shot free of the goal. Most younger players will have more success deflecting shots by using their open hands to slap the shot away from the goal.

- **Falling.** The proper technique of falling comes into play when the goalie has to dive for a shot outside of his reach. The main thing to remember in falling is that the whole body should go over as a unit. The best way to teach falling is to have players fall from a sitting position, then kneeling, then standing. First have your goalies sit on the ground. Have them fall over sideways, landing first on their hips and then fully on the ground, with their heads steady. Their bodies should immediately follow their hands or forearms to the ground. Players should use the ball to break their fall. Teaching the proper way to fall is usually most effectively done through a demonstration rather than an explanation. If you can get a high school or college goalie to show your players a good falling technique, that's ideal.

- **Outlet passes and kicking.** Goalkeepers need to learn how to make *outlet passes*, which are passes from the goalie to a defender, away from the goal and out to the side of the field. These are especially important for younger players, since most kids don't have the strength to kick the ball far enough out from the goal when kicking straight ahead. Drop kicks and punts are used to propel the ball farther down the field. In a *drop kick*, the goalie drops the ball to the ground, lets it bounce, and then immediately kicks it out of the goal. This is an important but difficult skill for a young player to learn, since the ball should barely touch the ground before the goalie kicks it out. Younger players can also punt the ball out. To *punt*, a player holds the ball with both hands, lets it fall, and then kicks it before it hits the ground, much as in football.

Getting Started

Positions and Formations

Positions can be very loose before kids play 11-on-11 games. Up until that point I like to play with a central defender and a central attacker. The rest of the positions are pretty free. Just talk about "getting wide," that is, using the full width of the field and not bunching in the middle. When we were kids playing our pick-up games, we sorted things out ourselves. As young players become more proficient, they will pick up how to play the different positions. My son Jamie literally played every position on the field, including goalie, during high school and college. I never worried about where he played, especially when he was a U-12 player.

Once the kids are into 11-on-11 full-field soccer, the easiest way to teach younger players formation play is through zones: defensive, midfield, and striking zones on the field. The best formation for play

```
                    goalkeep
                       g

                       d  sweeper
  d                    d              d
right back         center back     left back

  m                    m              m
right wing           center        left wing

  s                    s              s
right wing        center forward   left wing
```

defensive area

Once your players are into 11-on-11 play, the easiest way to teach formation play is through zones, with 4 defenders (not including goalie), 3 midfielders, and 3 strikers.

is a 4-3-3 format, which means you'll position 4 defenders, 3 midfielders, and 3 strikers in three distinct zones on the field.

1. **Defensive zone.** In the defensive zone you'll have four players to start an offensive attack. Perhaps the most important defensive player will be the *sweeper*, who stays between the rest of the defense and the goalkeeper and who will usually start most of the offensive attacks. Your sweeper should be one of your strongest players, someone who has a feel for the ball and is comfortable with it. If your sweeper can get the ball and build up from a controlled position—where the players are making good passes and are able to get their heads up—then chances are she will be able to start moving the ball up the field by passing.

   In addition to the sweeper are left, center, and right defenders, known as *left back, center back,* and *right back.* These players will *mark,* or keep track of, the corresponding forwards on the other team, but they shouldn't simply follow the opposing player all over the field. This tends to lead to a "gorilla mentality," where it becomes more a "me versus you" battle than deliberate team play. Rather, the defenders should cover the entire defensive zone, pulling the opposing forwards away from the sweeper, who is then free to bring the ball up to midfield.

2. **Midfield zone.** In the midfield are three players: the *left midfielder* on the left wing or side, the *center midfielder*, and the *right midfielder* on the right wing. The midfielders are the engine room of the team: they work in between the forwards and the defense to bring the ball up the field so that the forwards can score. Your midfielders need to be strong players with good skills. They will touch the ball often because at this age most players won't have the strength to knock the ball all the way from defense to the forwards.

3. **Attacking zone.** You should place three players in the attacking zone: a *left winger*, *center forward*, and *right winger*. The center forward is the striker, the person who moves through the middle of the attacking area. The other two are flank players. This is the easiest formation for young players to play. The center forward is a fast player who can make a run behind the defenders. The wingers can take the ball on the outside of the center forward in the flank, dribble, and *cross the ball*—pass it into the center of the attacking area. They need to have the same quickness as the center forward.

Another way to help younger children get a sense of positioning is to assign positions and give everyone a turn at trying them. Give each position a specific job: for example, when you assign a player a striker position, tell him, "You are our striker. You're going to have no defensive responsibilities. You're always going to be the person that's on the lookout, when we have the ball, for finding a space up front near the goal." Then give each player ten minutes or so to play that position. The players will all learn what each others' jobs are and will remember what to do when it's their turn to play.

Goal

The kid who wants to play goalie is the one who should take that position. If nobody wants to, then rotate everyone as goalie; also take turns if several people want to play in goal. Usually someone has an aptitude for diving and catching and will want to play in goal.

Teaching a Sense of Position with Six-on-Six

The best bet for teaching positioning is to use the discovery method with six-on-six (see the Discovery Method sidebar on page 16). Let the players play for a little while and see how they're starting to sort themselves out. Then call them in around you and ask what they see going on out on the field—how could they work together better? If the players don't come up with the right answers, direct them a little by suggesting they go wide to make an outlet for the ball, since it's so busy in the middle of the field. Ask them what happens when the other team gets the ball and how their own team could prevent the other team from scoring. You'll be surprised at how quickly your players will come up with answers and solutions to the problems on their own.

Some Notes on Defending

One of the biggest differences between soccer and other court sports such as basketball is that when on defense, the soccer player has to give equal attention to both the ball and her "man," the opponent playing in the corresponding part of the field. Soccer players have to move, follow the ball, and watch their opponents—all at the same time.

If you are coaching younger players, you shouldn't spend much time during practice trying to teach them the principles of defending. They are too young to fully understand the principles and won't be able to focus on those skills in isolation. Rather, make suggestions while they are playing.

The best time to work on defending skills is during one-on-one drills. Give your players specific skills to focus on. For example, when the ball is played, have the defender try to step in and win the ball before the attacker has received it. A good defender can look at the person who is going to play the ball, can anticipate the pass, and can intercept it. If the attacker does get the ball, the defender has to assess how the attacker has received it: Has he made a bad first touch? Is there an opportunity to get the ball off the attacker's foot? If the attacker is in control and the defender can't get the ball, then the defender has to dictate to the attacker which way he can go—he can put the attacker onto his weak foot or can allow him into an area with little or no space.

Throw-ins

As discussed in chapter 2, when the ball goes out of bounds along a sideline and a member of the opposing team touched it last, any player on your team throws the ball back into play. Throw-ins are a simple procedure and can be addressed in one of the early sessions. It is not something I would spend much time on. Most youth referees do not penalize for technique that is slightly off, but you will want your players to learn the proper technique. The ball must be held with two hands and thrown from behind and over the head. The player arches her back, brings her weight onto her leading leg, and whips her body forward as she releases the ball. Both feet must remain on the ground throughout the throw. Throw-ins could be incorporated as part of a warm up in an early practice.

Kicks

The various kicks for penalties and out-of-bounds situations (corner kicks, free kicks, and penalty kicks, as discussed under Out of Bounds on page 18) should be taken by whoever normally performs them well. If it is not a crucial kick, you might give it to a player who does not often handle the ball or score. Or if there are several good kickers, a rotation system might be the solution. A corner kick is tricky to execute, so usually the player who is best at it takes them—or in some cases whoever can!

How to Teach Formation Play

Games such as Two-Zone Soccer (game 55 page 117) and Three-Zone Soccer (game 56 page 117)—which are essentially miniature soccer games

One-on-one drills are the best time to work on defending skills. Give your players specific skills to focus on. The player on the left has just intercepted the pass.

that are slanted in favor of defense and that force players to pass—will prepare your team for three-zone (defense, middle, and attack), full-field soccer. These games can be difficult to learn at first and require that your players are comfortable in three-on-one situations. If they aren't yet at this stage, start them on minigames that create three-on-one situations, such as Piggy in the Middle (game 32 on page 107), a simple keep-away game in which three players pass the ball around a single player trying to intercept the ball. Players should advance from Piggy in the Middle to a game like Target Man (game 54 on page 116), where three defenders face off against a single attacker in each half of the field. Let your players be your guide—if they are frustrated and not having fun, you're pushing too hard. Once they do understand these concepts, however, their understanding of the game will increase dramatically.

Give Your Players Space

When your players are learning to play in zones, it is a good idea to make the field as large as they can reasonably manage. A wider field will give them more room in which to spread out and will create good supporting passing angles—where players without the ball move to create easy passes for the ball-handler. Remember, though, that younger and smaller players will have trouble making passes if the field is too wide. Widen or narrow the field according to the age and ability of your team.

Basic Ingredients of a Good Soccer Team

The first ingredient of a good team is that the players have fun playing the game. The second is that they have fun playing together.

If the players are having fun and enjoying healthy competition, they will want to improve their techniques and understanding of the game. Once this is established, the rest will fall into place. Kids love to compete, so keep them competing. Let the games do the coaching. Winning will be important to the kids, but it should never be too high on the priority list of the youth coach.

The Practice

This practice template is designed to be used throughout the season. It outlines a basic structure of activities, with specific time allotments, for you to follow during your practices, covering all aspects of the game.

Preparation Is Key

Before every practice, work out a lesson plan and decide on the objectives of each session. The aim of the first practice should be to get to know your players and have them get to know you. You also need to set up and introduce your standards of discipline—not through words, since it usually does no good to talk about these issues with the kids, although you may have

The first day's emphasis should be on fun, but keep the players under control.

already had this discussion with the parents. The first day of practice is where you will establish discipline standards through actions—through drills and forfeits and games.

Remember that the goal for the first day should be to have a good time, but you should also be bringing your players under control while you're doing it. Put them out on the field, bring them back around you, over and over again—don't let them out too far. Think of this initial coaching day as like riding a horse: the first time out, don't let the reins drop and the horse gallop. You need to keep the reins fairly tight at the beginning; as things build over the session and the horse starts to get to know you, then you can loosen up and let it gallop a bit. Don't let your kids gallop too early.

Map out what you'll do at the first practice, and get out on the field early to prepare yourself. To avoid getting bogged down in the administrative details of beginning a new season, make sure your team manager is available at the first practice to answer such questions about where to get equipment, what to do if the weather's bad, and with whom Sally can carpool on Thursdays. You need to concentrate on the coaching end of things, so let someone else handle the other bits and pieces.

Get cones for drills and games set up beforehand—once the practice is underway, you don't want to interrupt the tempo and flow of the drills by running around trying to set up new drills. It is ideal to set up the entire field beforehand so you can go quickly and easily from one drill to the next.

Format for Practice

It is important to have a consistent format for every practice. Like all routines, setting up a structure for practices helps in many ways: it gets the kids into habits and into a good pattern where they know what to expect. It will also help you down the line to establish when the next activity should start. There should be flexibility within the routine, but the structure really should remain consistent.

Because there is so much for young players to learn about the sport of soccer, try to keep the technical skills sections devoted to one particular skill each session, such as passing, defending, shooting, and heading. Try also to emphasize the more aggressive skills such as heading and shooting at practices that are closer to games. For example, if you have two practices per week with a game on Saturday, your emphasis for the first practice of the week might be on passing and for the second practice it might be shooting.

The following format template will take you through a 90-minute session. If you have less or more practice time, you can adjust the individual segments according to your needs.
- gathering activity: 15 minutes prior to practice and 5 minutes into it
- fun warm-up without the ball: 10 minutes

Try to keep the technical skills sections devoted to one particular skill each session, such as ball handling. Here, players work on keeping their heads up while controlling the ball.

- ball handling and control: 30 minutes
- technical skills: 15 minutes
- game—competition: 20 minutes
- doggy bag and final meeting: 10 minutes

Gathering Activity

Start the gathering activity perhaps 15 minutes before practice starts—often the first kids on your team will begin arriving at this time, and you don't want them just standing around. Have a little "field" set up so that the first four kids or so can have a two-on-two game going. As the other kids arrive, place them in two-on-two or three-on-three games. Young kids don't need a lot of stretching, so normally they can begin playing immediately. Keep this going for at least 5 minutes into the practice, so that all of the late kids will have arrived. Then bring players in around you, giving them time for a quick drink. Always have the kids bring their own water bottles to practice.

When you bring your players together, let them know that the practice will always begin with the gathering exercise. You may find that kids come earlier and earlier so that they can play the game before practice. It's a nice gathering activity and will help the kids get started playing games, learning skills, and having fun. This is not a coaching time—this is a time where the kids discover their own game and have fun. Another benefit of the gathering exercise is that it gets them going and gives you a chance to have a bit of time to get your last-minute thoughts together before practice. There are many other gathering activities—but none that are better for soccer than actually playing a game.

Warm-Up (10 minutes)

Put the balls aside for now, so that you can have a fun warm-up that emphasizes body control and quick thinking. One of the best ways to warm up for soccer is through chasing games, such as Caterpillar or Odd Man Out (see games 3 and 4 on pages 97 and 98). You can have chasing games in ones, twos, threes, fours, or chains of as many kids as you want. Chasing games don't require a lot of skill apart from paying attention to the boundaries of the field and having your wits about you, but they help teach important skills for soccer: thinking, running, chasing, covering an opponent, and concentrating on the surrounding action, all at the same time. You may find that the quickest-thinking players on the team are often some of your best players.

This warm-up should be a time where everyone is just moving around, having a good bit of fun, and it doesn't usually need to last much longer than 10 minutes. That short time sets the tone for the rest of the practice—fun and movement.

Ball Handling and Control (30 minutes)

For young players, their first opponent is always going to be the ball. Until they can overcome and control the ball, it's going to be difficult for them to take on opponents. That's why the ball-handling component of the practice is the longest, usually 30 minutes or so. Keep in mind that much of this time is spent on little games that help reinforce the skills. You'll repeatedly move from coaching points to a game and back again. With this format, players will be learning a particular skill and will also be competing with each other much of the time.

Technical Skills (15 minutes)

The technical training part of the practice is where you add another skill, such as passing, heading, shooting, and other various aspects of the game.

When you are working on a skill, especially a complicated one, break it up into smaller components so that you don't need to stop and do a lot of explaining at one stretch. Get your players going, give some more instruction, and get them going again. You won't get the skill perfect in one session—don't try to. Work at it a little, get in a few points, make a note of how far you got, and next time try to take it a little bit further. You aren't going to teach your players how to pass in one session—it'll take them a lifetime. Go back to the very basics each time and build on the players' current knowledge. The better they get, the quicker you can go through the basics. The younger or more novice the players, the more time you'll spend on the basics. Even the international players go back to the basics every time they practice—they just don't spend time relearning these skills.

Game (20 minutes)

Always finish off with a game. At this final part of the session there's not a lot of teaching going on—let your players play the game and be competitive. Just by allowing them to compete against each other, you're teaching them how to handle winning and losing. They will learn what it's like to win and to try hard to win. Players need to learn how to win and lose well. When they play their game on Saturday, it's important that they can handle themselves with dignity whether they're winners or losers.

So make these games a competition: arrange your players on teams, let the teams win and lose, and at the end of the day don't do too much coaching. You can comment, of course. If you're playing multiple small teams, you could bring your players in around you at the changeover and

Always finish off practice with a game—let your team play and be competitive.

offer a few points. That's how they will improve. But remember that at the first practice you'll most likely be just creating the structure for future practice games. You'll need to determine how many kids play per side, whether it is three a side, or four or five a side. You'll also have to work out who will play whom. Is it going to be four teams of four, will the two winners play, and the two losers play, or do you play round robin where all the teams play one another? These are the little things that you want to establish during your first session so that players know what to expect. Change the mixture of players and numbers on each side for variety.

Doggy Bag and Final Meeting (10 minutes)

Kids like the idea of being given a project to work on when they aren't at practice. Take something out of the session that maybe wasn't done as well as you would like or that simply needs more practice, and give it as homework. Since most kids don't like the word *homework*, call it their "doggy bag." Demonstrate a skill that players worked on earlier in the practice—ball handling, for example—and talk about it. You might say, "We need to work on ball handling. Let's see if we can all take this one home with us and chew on it and see when we come back for next week's practice if we can get it a little better." It's a good way to get players to practice skills that are difficult for them, and it keeps them involved with the sport when they aren't at practice.

You set up the drill, and then you ask the players to identify what you're looking for. Bring out the dialogue from them. As long as they are consistent in the words they use, they can make up their own soccer vocabulary that works for all of you. It's important that your team develops its own vocabulary. The key points are that everyone understands the vocabulary you'll be using and that you all discover it together.

The great thing about the discovery method is that all the players are concentrating on what is in front of them. You ask them the question before the demonstration so you are leading them to the important concept of the skill, but they discover it for themselves. Children (and adults) have a much greater chance of remembering things that they discover themselves. Don't spoon-feed them—let them discover.

CHAPTER 6

Sample Practices

This chapter outlines several sample practices, covering all levels of play from beginner to more advanced. Watch your players carefully during practice to monitor their success with any given drill game. You'll need to use your judgment about how they're doing, and sometimes you'll need to fiddle with the drills, making adjustments that cater to their particular ability level. Some eight-year-olds can handle a three-on-one drill, and some twelve-year-olds can't. A coach will soon know how her kids are doing if she moves slowly. As your team progresses in skills and experience, you can replace the drills outlined in these five practices with other drills found in chapter 9. All games covered here are explained in greater detail in chapter 9 where they are numbered consecutively. Those numbers appear in boxes next to drill names for ease of reference.

Basic Beginning Practice

This practice is great for all levels of play. For younger players who are just learning the game, you may want to use this practice for the entire season. Older, more experienced players might benefit from this review during the early part of the season. The emphasis here is on introducing and working on fundamental skills, with a focus on dribbling and passing.

Gathering Activity

The small, informal soccer games recommended as an activity as players arrive (see chapter 5) can stay constant throughout the season: playing a game of soccer is the most fundamental way to teach and practice the skills of the game, and it's something every kid enjoys—it's why they are on the team. Your players will also appreciate the routine provided by a consistent gathering activity. They'll know that as soon as they come to practice they can start playing and moving. The benefit for you is that from the moment your players arrive, they are involved in improving their skills, with nobody hanging around.

Warm-Up
Stuck in the Mud   1
This variation on freeze tag is a simple game that not only gives the kids a chance to get moving but also makes them think ahead. They have to figure out how to "unstick" their teammates without getting caught themselves. (See game 1 on page 97.)

Ball Handling
One of the keys to successfully moving with the ball is to get your players to dribble with their heads up. It's important to encourage your players to get the ball out from under their feet. Young players tend to want to touch the ball often while they are dribbling, so they keep it much closer to their bodies than they need to. This makes it difficult for them to pay attention to what's happening on the field around them. The best way to teach heads-up soccer is to play games that require your players to keep their eyes and attention on the field or the coach, rather than looking down at the ball.

The ball should be about a foot in front of the player as she dribbles, but this distance between the player and ball always depends on how fast the player is moving: if she is running down the field, the ball will be farther away than if she is dribbling slowly.

Play games that require your players to keep their eyes and attention on the field or the coach, not the ball.

Moving with the Ball

When your players move forward with the ball, they should always be touching it with the laces of their shoes. They should dribble the ball on the move with a normal running style, not with their feet out like a penguin or Charlie Chaplin. When they turn to the inside, they should use the inside of the foot to move the ball. When they turn to the outside, they should use the outside of the foot. Introduce the concept of *moving with the ball* (dribbling) by asking them questions: "How do you move with the ball? Which part of the foot do you move? Which part of the foot do you use to turn the ball?" Have them answer the questions and then try out their hypotheses on the field. Then bring them back in around you and ask your questions again. The kids will pick this up quickly. Some of your players will get the answers right away. Use them to demonstrate the proper technique and then let everyone try it again.

Spaceman 14

In this game players aim to distribute themselves evenly within an area of the field while dribbling. The drill helps players work on controlling the ball with their heads up, while at the same time they must be aware of the space on the field. (See game 14 on page 100.)

Finger Game 11

In this drill players dribble the ball, but at the same time they must watch you to determine how many fingers you are holding up. This game teaches players to dribble with their heads up. (See game 11 on page 100.)

Truck and Trailer Game 13

One player dribbling a ball has to closely follow a teammate who is also dribbling a ball. Although it sounds simple, kids of all levels can enjoy this game, and it can be quite difficult to accomplish well. The goal is for your players to hone their ball-control skills so that they can easily follow a player directly in front of them without losing control of the ball. (See game 13 on page 100.)

Technical Skill: Passing

The most basic and common pass is the simple, inside-of-the-foot pass. The two most important aspects of learning a simple pass are direction—passing it to the right person—and the pace, or speed, of the ball. The biggest problem for most youngsters when they first learn to pass is their lack of control over how hard or how soft they hit the ball. Divide your players into pairs and have them work on passing the ball back and forth as softly as possible while still traveling the distance between partners.

The next thing to look at when they pass is how they are using their feet. In a good pass the foot is firm, and the toe is up. Bring your players in around you and ask, "Which part of the foot do I use when I pass the ball?" Listen to their answers and use either your assistant or a player who does this well to demonstrate proper foot position. Ask this person questions

Split players into pairs and have them work on passing the ball back and forth as softly as possible.

about the way she is using her foot. "Is your toe up or down?" Ask the group, "Is her foot firm, or is it a wet fish?"

The "wet fish" question is great for engaging the players in the discussion. It gets them thinking about what they think a wet fish looks like and comparing what the proper foot position versus a "wet fish" position would look like. Get them to tell you what a "wet fish" foot looks like, and use their answers to demonstrate the differences between improper and proper foot position.

Send your players out onto the field again to pass to their partners, working on soft passing and no wet fish. When you're watching them say, "Hey, I want a toe up. I don't want any wet fish." Be aware that they will be able to manage this foot position for only five minutes or so, and it won't be perfect. Don't go for perfection right away, since it isn't going to happen. Players need to know that once they've done some serious work, what follows will be a fun game.

Soccer Marbles Game 24
In this game each player's ball is a "marble," and they shoot and try to hit these marbles. The drill will help your players work on their passing accuracy. (See game 24 on page 105.)

Concluding Game

This is the time where you divide your team in half and just play the game. Or, you might want to set up two or three three-on-three games or two four-on-four games, depending on the number of players. It's important to finish up practice by letting them play, letting them work on the skills they have been learning throughout practice, without too much coaching. It's good to praise the skills you've been working on that they do well—for example, when someone makes a good pass and has good foot position—since it sets an example for the other players. But don't spend time correcting what isn't working as well. A few simple reminders are all you should do here, since the game will be teaching them.

During the concluding game, you can put conditions on what happens. For example, if you've been working on passing during the technical session, make the condition during the game that after one team scores, that team can't score again until the other team does. They should work to keep possession of the ball every time they get it, while the other team continues to try to score a goal. This will teach the players that when they are a goal up they should not necessarily be looking for goals, but they should focus on retaining possession of the ball—which is tremendous for promoting a passing game. Limiting the goals prevents one team from scoring too many goals—the most any team is ever going to win the game by is one goal—and it forces the team in the lead to work hard at retaining possession.

Doggy Bag

You will have to decide at the end of every session what your players need to work on most. This will become apparent as you get to know your players and how well they pick up the skills you are teaching them. For this first practice, call your players together and stress how well they've done this first day. As a doggy bag, have them work on moving with the ball, concentrating on controlling the ball with the laces of their feet. (See Doggy Bag section, page 56.)

End practice with a team cheer—have your players excited about what they've just done and looking forward to the next practice.

Advanced Beginner Practice

The emphasis of today's practice is on finishing.

Gathering Activity

This will remain the same at every practice. Make sure you've set up a few minifields with the cones for a few three-on-three or four-on-four games so that kids can join in as soon as they get to the field. Call them in around you about 5 minutes after practice is supposed to start.

Pairs Chasing is a freeze-tag game that teaches teamwork.

Warm-Up

Pairs Chasing   2

This is a freeze-tag game where players are interlocked in pairs. They can link up in various arrangements: with one arm on each other's shoulder or, to make it more complicated, they can link arms with one player facing forward and the other facing backward. (See game 2 on page 97.)

Ball Handling and Control

Change Game   10

Send your players out on the field, each dribbling a ball. At your signal, each player has to stop his ball, leave it, and race to acquire someone else's ball. This competitive game helps your players with ball-handling skills, maintaining space on the field, and keeping their heads up. (See game 10 on page 99.)

Keepy Up   35

Keepy Up, or juggling, is the most important game for learning ball control. What's great about it is that the kids can do it almost anywhere, on their own, at their own level. Start with what I call one touch/one bounce: the player drops the ball and touches it with her instep (where the laces of the shoe are), lets it bounce on the ground, touches it again with her instep, lets it bounce on the ground, and keeps this sequence going as long as possible. As players advance, increase the number of touches between bounces and add other body surfaces. (See game 35 on page 109.)

Turns and Spins   16

This drill teaches players to turn the ball, first by slowing it on the sole of the foot and then by spinning it on the outside or inside of the foot while turning. (See game 16 on page 101.)

King of the Ring   18

At the end of these two progressions—Keepy Up and Turns and Spins—finish with a fun and simple game that reinforces ball handling and control. In King of the Ring, players dribble within a defined area, simultaneously trying to kick each other's balls out of the area and to maintain control of their own ball. This is a great game for learning the fundamentals of soccer because it incorporates ball-handling skills and the concept of being aware of what's going on around you. (See game 18 on page 102.)

Technical Skill: Passing and Receiving

Pass and Receive, Head Up   25

In a correct pass reception, both the foot and the head come up. If a player can control the ball in one touch, his head comes up immediately after reception. The more time a player spends looking down at the ball, the less time his head is up to see what the other players are doing and to make a decision. This drill teaches your players "heads-up soccer." (See game 25 on page 105.)

Technical Skill: Shooting

Straight Shots at Goal   36

For the first shooting session, focus just on straight shots. First demonstrate a straight shot at the goal. Then divide players into pairs and have them strike the ball to their partners from the ground. (See game 36 on page 109.)

Target Shooting   37

In this drill two players face one another about 25 yards apart with a target—a cone or ball—midway between them. Challenge them to hit the

---

When Some Kids Get It, and Some Don't

Usually you'll have a team where some of the kids pick up the skills very quickly, and others take much longer. To keep the advanced kids interested while you are helping the kids who need more practice for a particular skill, add one extra component to the basic skill for the advanced players to work on. You'll make two coaching points, and you'll keep everyone interested in the drill.

A Story Brings Home the Skill

When teaching kids how to do various skills, I find that the most effective way to get them to understand and remember the concept is by creating a picture or scenario. For example, when I teach kids about turns, I say, "I don't like Queen Mary turns." Most of these kids will have no idea who or what Queen Mary refers to, but when you explain that the *Queen Mary* was one of the big ocean liners that used to sail between Europe and North America, they form a picture in their minds. Then you say, "How does that ocean liner turn? Does it turn quickly, or does it turn slowly?" They'll usually tell you, "It turns slowly." And I'll respond, "I don't want Queen Mary turns—I want speedboat turns. How does a speedboat turn?" Right away they'll tell or show you how quickly a jet ski or a speedboat turns. Then they make the connection between a speedboat and a soccer player: when soccer players turn, they don't turn slowly—they turn quickly.

Similarly, when we play King of the Ring, I tell them, "You've got two jobs with your feet. It's like walking along the streets of New York City with your wallet in your back pocket. You're a pickpocket and you're looking to pick someone else's pocket, but at the same time, you're being very careful that nobody picks your own pocket. On the soccer field, you're trying to kick someone else's ball, but you've got to watch out because you've got your own ball. And although you're trying to gang up and sneak up on someone else's ball, you've got to always be watching your back." Kids love the mental pictures, and they understand the concepts better when they are explained this way.

target by striking the ball straight. This drill develops accuracy and control in shooting. (See game 37 on page 110.)

Tippee-Onee   39

After playing the target game for a few points, finish this technical session with a game of Tippee-Onee. Your players will remain in pairs approximately 25 yards apart, and each pair will have a small, 6- to 7-yard goal area at either end of the space. One player tries to score a goal on her partner. The defender is allowed one touch (this is where the one-tippee comes in) to either catch the ball as a goalkeeper or control the ball. If she can control it with that one touch, she can then return a quick running shot. (See game 39 on page 110.)

Concluding Game

See the description of the concluding game on page 55.

Doggy Bag

A fun doggy bag for this practice might be to practice Turns and Spins (see game 16 on page 101). Kids can work on this by themselves, and they will enjoy improving their "moves." Ball-handling skills require a lot of practice, and their confidence will soar as they become more comfortable maneuvering the ball.

Intermediate Practice

The emphasis of today's practice is on defending.

Gathering Activity

See the description of the gathering activity on page 53.

Warm-Up

Caterpillar   3

This is a fast-moving tag game in which players are grouped in chains of three or more. It teaches players to coordinate their movements as a team and requires quick thinking. (See game 3 on page 97.)

Odd Man Out   4

Here is another tag game involving groups of connected players. Three players link arms, with the middle person facing backward. As in Caterpillar, this awkward arrangement forces players to move as a team and think on their feet. (See game 4 on page 98.)

Triangle Tag   5

In this game three players link arms and try to protect the center player from being tagged. This game teaches players to move and guard one another. (See game 5 on page 98.)

Snake Tag   6

This is a variation on Triangle Tag in which the player on the end of the chain of three requires protection. (See game 6 on page 98.)

In Snake Tag, the player on the end of the chain of three requires protection, in this instance from the player at left.

Getting Even Teams When Scrimmaging

An easy way to divide your players into two teams of equal ability is to have your players choose partners. Players of like ability generally tend to gravitate toward one another. After they've paired up, split the partners, placing half the pairs on one team and the other half on a second team. You may have to shift one or two players to even things out, but this method usually creates two fairly equal teams.

Ball Handling

Sharks and Minnows 17

In this game a couple of players without balls try to steal the balls that the rest of the players are dribbling. This game is fun and great for working on ball-handling skills and for heads-up soccer. (See game 17 on page 102.)

Ball Control

Keepy Up 35

Once your players can handle 20 consecutive one touch/one bounce sequences, start them on a two touches/one bounce game. Have them alternate feet for their touches. (See game 35 on page 109.)

Fighting Roosters is ideal for working on ball-handling skills and teaching players how to defend the ball.

When Drills Start to Drag

If you find your players' interest in a drill is starting to drag, and they are fooling around or getting distracted, get their attention refocused by stopping the drill and checking the score. For example, if they are playing Catch the Tiger's Tail, call out, "Halftime," and go around the group, asking what the score is. Tell everyone that if there is no score or a tie score when you call out, "Game over," both players on the team have to do a forfeit. Losers of the game also have to do the forfeit. This will immediately get your players back into a competitive spirit.

Technical Skill: Handling Pressure

Fighting Roosters 52

This game is ideal for working on ball-handling skills and teaching players how to defend the ball when an opponent is pressuring. Players are grouped in pairs according to similar ability. Each player dribbles a ball. One player tries to touch her partner's ball without losing control of her own. This game doesn't work well until your players have achieved a certain level of ball control. (See game 52 on page 114.)

Catch the Tiger's Tail 53

This is the next progression from Fighting Roosters. It is a similar game, but this time two players must use one ball, which is the tiger's tail. The person who doesn't have the ball tries to touch the ball with his foot—to catch the tiger's tail. (See game 53 on page 115.)

Concluding Game

See the description of the concluding game on page 55.

Doggy Bag

A doggy bag for this practice might be to practice a variety of spin turns. Have your players work on their spinouts (using the outside of the foot), spin-ins (using the inside of the foot), and Rivelino (step-over moves, see page 33).

Advanced Intermediate Practice

The emphasis in this practice is on heading.

Gathering Activity

See the description of the gathering activity on page 53.

Warm-Up

Relays

I set up relay races that take very little technical ability but require a good bit of teamwork and cooperation and a lot of energy. Put players in lines and have them run relay races out to a marker and back. Incorporate variations such as hopping, skipping, and ball handling.

Ball Handling

Remember to always review what you've worked on in previous practices before moving on to a completely new skill. If your players are having trouble picking up the skills, go back to what you've worked on in the first three practices. If they are ready to move on to a new skill, first go over the ones they know and then move on. You could do Spaceman at the beginning of every practice, for example, and each time they will learn something new and hone their ball-handling skills.

Spaceman   14
See game 14 on page 100.

Truck and Trailer Game   13
See game 13 on page 100.

King of the Ring   18
See game 18 on page 102.

Ball Control
Keepy Up   35
Once a player has mastered Keepy Up with two touches/one bounce, he can try the Keepy-Up Ladder. This is simply when the player starts with 20 sequences of one touch/one bounce, goes to two touches and a bounce, moves on to three touches and a bounce, and keeps adding on a touch every time, until he hits 10 touches. If the player misses one of his touches, he goes back to the first step on the ladder and starts climbing up again. (See game 35 on page 109.)

Technical Skill: Heading
Glasgow Kisses   41
Glasgow Kisses are, literally, head butts. In this drill, have each player stand and hold a ball. First have the players gently head the ball up in the air and catch it. Then tell them you want them to give the ball a Glasgow Kiss. They'll enjoy the challenge of "smacking" the ball and will overcome their tendency to shrink away from it. (See game 41 on page 111.)

Heading Ladder   42
The best way to practice heading is to have each player throw the ball into the air, head it once, and then catch it. Once they have mastered that, challenge them to head the ball twice before catching it, then three times, and so forth. Move up the "heading ladder"—increasing the number of head

The best way to practice heading is to have your players throw the ball into the air, head it once, and then catch it.

bounces between catches—until the ladder breaks. Then they go back down to rung one. As with Keepy Up, this drill works well with pairs. (See game 42 on page 111.)

Concluding Game

See the description of the concluding game on page 55.

Doggy Bag

Have your players work on their Heading Ladders. Remind them to strike at the ball with their heads rather than letting the ball come to them, and to keep their eyes open and their mouths closed.

Advanced Practice

The emphasis of this practice is again on passing.

Gathering Activity

See the description of the gathering activity on page 53.

Warm-up

See the description of the warm-up on page 54.

Chain Tag   8

This simple tag game begins with a single chaser. The first person tagged begins a chain with the chaser, and the chain lengthens as more players are

The Truth about the Dangers of Heading

Many parents are concerned about heading, worried that their child will suffer a head injury. Soccer is a fast-moving, sometimes rough-and-tumble game, and although kids can get banged up a bit, heading is not an inherently dangerous aspect of the game. A soccer ball is a reasonably soft object, and proper heading technique teaches players to meet the ball rather than be hit by it. It *is* possible to bloody a nose or lip, or perhaps even to get a concussion. But this is highly unlikely. The key to avoiding injury in any part of a sport is by mastering the fundamentals of proper technique, and heading is no exception.

tagged. This is an effective warm-up that teaches cooperation and team-work. (See game 8 on page 99.)

Ball Handling

Fighting Roosters 52
See game 52 on page 114.

Catch the Tiger's Tail 53
See game 53 on page 115.

One-on-One Soccer 19

All of the previous games have been leading up to One-on-One Soccer: short, intense games between two players. All of the skills your players have learned so far will come into play here. One-on-one games are very tiring, so it's a good idea to let a game go for about a minute and then stop the players and make your coaching points. (See game 19 on page 103.)

You can teach your players just a few specific moves that they can name for themselves. A classic soccer move is beating another player by a quick change of direction. Or you can demonstrate just how easily the person in control of the ball can slow down and then speed up suddenly. Another move is to change both direction and speed.

Learning—and Naming—Individual Moves

Once you've reached the level of one-on-one games, you can start to bring some progressions into ball handling. You've played Spaceman, worked on turns, spins, and changing balls. Now you can introduce moves and have your players name them. One of the first individual moves you can teach your players is a *step-over*. In this move the player steps across the ball with one foot, immediately turns around and puts his foot on top of the ball and moves away in another direction. This is a great turn, a change of direction that's quite deceptive. I always call this move the *Rivelino* because it was originated by a famous Brazilian player named Rivelino. But when you introduce this move to your players, let them come up with a name that's familiar and meaningful to them. Maybe they are familiar with local players, or teams, and want to name it after them. One of the best ways to find a name is to use the name of someone on the team. As you're practicing a new move, demonstrate it and then say, "Hey, look at Billy Brown. We'll call this the brownie!" So suddenly this move becomes the *brownie*.

As you start your ball-handling segment, introduce the idea of getting away from defenders, and ask your players how they could move differently to accomplish this. "Hey, can we change direction quickly and get away quickly? Can we change speed? Can we slow down and speed up?" Bring these different facets into the warm-up, the first part of the session with the ball. Introduce the moves and then finish with the one-on-one games so the kids have a chance to try out the new concept.

Technical Skill: Passing and Receiving
Triangle Game   26
In this game a pair of players passes the ball back and forth through a triangle made from three cones (or balls or pinnies). Each side of the triangle should be two or three yards long. One player has to pass the ball through the cone triangle and out the other side without it touching any of the cones. His partner has to receive the ball and pass it back through a different side of the triangle. The ball can never be played back through the same side twice in a row. By adding a second pair of players and keeping score, you can make the game competitive. This game helps players learn to pass and receive the ball properly. (See game 26 on page 105.)

Triangle Game Progression   27
In this version of the Triangle Game, your players will be working with the different surfaces of their feet to receive the ball through the triangle. You can specify, for example, that players use the outside or the inside of their feet, or that they receive the ball with the right foot, cross it over, and return the pass with the left. (See game 27 on page 106.)

Multigoal Game   29
Divide your players into pairs. Set up a series of goals about one or two yards apart in the 30-by-30-yard practice area, with as many goals as there are pairs. Each pair of players has 30 seconds in which to see how many goals they can score. They can go to each goal only once, and they may not play at a goal another pair is already playing, so they have to look for a goal that's empty. This game will get your players passing, looking around the field, and coordinating with their partners. (See game 29 on page 106.)

Ball Control
Keepy Up   35
As the players' confidence in their ball-control abilities grows, you can introduce the thigh, chest, and head as alternative surfaces of control. Different parts of the foot, the inside or even the heel, can be introduced for the strongest players. As the players improve in control, they can also begin doing the same exercises in pairs, juggling the ball back and forth between them. When starting Keepy Up in pairs, follow the same progression up

from one touch/one bounce, gradually increasing the number of touches between bounces. (See game 35 on page 109.)

Concluding Game

See the description of the concluding game on page 55.

Doggy Bag

Have your players practice the triangle game at home, with a friend, sibling, or parent. Challenge the kids to invent their own moves, as well as practicing the ones you introduced.

Questions and Answers

Q. The first practice was a nightmare. Even though I wrote out a practice plan, things just fell apart. I couldn't get a sense of how long to keep going on the drills—some of the kids mastered them quickly and seemed to lose interest, while others never really got it. I kept moving things along to accommodate the better kids, but I felt the less-skilled ones didn't get enough time on things. How do I address this for next time?

A. Kids aren't all going to get it the first day. The key to coaching beginners or young players is to revise, revise, revise. Take the skills you taught the first day and do them again, maybe adding on one new thing at the end. Never start with all new skills each practice, assuming that since they did them once they'll remember and do them perfectly. Some days practice just won't be good—it happens to every coach. Evaluate what you're doing, and keep the practice moving along. Remember that the better players will pair up with each other, just as the less-skilled players will pair up. The better-skilled players will usually manage to keep themselves amused, and although the less-skilled ones may not be getting the skill, it doesn't mean they still aren't having fun. At your next practice go back and do it all again, discovering what works and what doesn't—that's half the fun of coaching.

Q. I have had the good luck to get a group of kids who seem to really pick up the skills quickly. We have had two practices, and I have found that the kids are going through the blocks more quickly than the time I've allotted. They are getting bored, and I'm left with a big chunk of time at the end with nothing to do. How should I address this?

A. Some kids will pick stuff up very quickly. If so, spend more time on the game side of practice. Let them play soccer so that the skills they are practicing are more competitive. Most of the drills in this book will be done by international players, so they are applicable to all

Avoiding the "Pick Me! Pick Me!" Syndrome

When you choose players for teams or for demonstrations, you can avoid the inevitable hand waving and shouting of "Pick me!" by announcing that you will be picking the quietest, most well-behaved players for the team or the drill.

levels of play. Keep the tempo going, make every game competitive, and they'll enjoy what they're doing.

Q. We've had three practices, and while the kids are enjoying themselves, they just aren't getting the skills. I've been trying to build on what we've done from the previous practice, but I feel like I have to keep reteaching the basics each time. Do I keep trying to move on, or just start all over again?

A. Revisit the basic skills. Always go over what you did previously, and you'll find that with some kids you'll have to go over everything every time. This is fine—soccer is a game for life, and one that can't be mastered in just a few practices. The kids will have fun playing, no matter what they are doing, as long as you keep it upbeat and a game.

Q. My team is ready for more complicated skill drills. We've already mastered the ones in the book. What do I do now?

A. Use your imagination. These drills should keep you going throughout the season. Make them more competitive, look for a higher standard for every drill than you have before—better passing, better heading, better ball handling.

Q. All through practice my players bug me about when they will get a chance to scrimmage. Would it hurt to just let them scrimmage for an entire practice every so often?

A. No! In fact, it's a great idea to have your players come out and just play. A good way to teach skills while just playing a game is what I call the "whole-part-whole" method. Use the game as a gathering activity, and then take a piece of the game to focus on, such as passing. Talk about how to work on making better passes, and then let the players go back to the game again. You can do this for many skills, and the procedure will teach a lot. One thing to keep in mind is that many young players won't have the stamina to play a game the entire length of practice, so plan rest activities throughout.

Q. I have a couple of players who are much better than the others. Their parents have come to me after practice to complain about the amount of time I spend teaching skills that they feel are too "basic" for their children. How do I address this?

A. Your best bet is to pair up the exceptional kids. They should work on honing their skills—just as all the other players should work on honing their skills—and they can challenge each other. You may want to give them special doggy bags, or take some extra time at the end of each practice to show them a special skill they can work on outside of practice.

CHAPTER 7

Game Time

The first game of the season can be both an exciting and intimidating time—you may find that those butterflies you used to get when you were a kid have come back with a vengeance. This game is the first test of how well all of your team's hard work will pay off, and you may consider the first game as a test of your coaching ability, as well. Remember, though, that while it is easy to judge yourself solely on the end score, one team has to win and the other has to lose—it's up to you to recognize and appreciate the skills and sportsmanship your players exhibit on the field, regardless of the outcome.

Rules of the Game

Set an Example

The most important role you'll play in the game will be as an example to your players. You will need to prepare yourself, to visualize your behavior and actions during the game, to control your anxiety and excitement. No matter how much you talk to your players about good sportsmanship and the importance of respecting authority, your actions are going to speak much more about what you really believe than what you say.

Arrive Early and Be Prepared

If your first game is an away game, plan on arriving at your destination about 45 minutes before kickoff. This will give you plenty of time to get organized and allows you extra time before your players arrive. If it's a home game, you should get to the field about 40 minutes before the game to make sure that everything is ready for the game. Have your players meet at the field approximately 30 minutes before every game to begin their warm-up. Coordinate with your team manager who will be responsible for equipment for the game such as flags, goal nets, and game sheet.

A calm, positive attitude is contagious. Let the kids know how you feel.

When your players arrive, don't start talking about the game right away—keep the atmosphere fun and as close to normal as possible. Players will be feeling the excitement of game day as much or more than you are, and you need to keep that energy under control. Check to make sure that they all have their water bottles and their uniforms. It is a good idea to carry spare uniforms with you, in case a player has forgotten his or one gets torn during a game. Let them play their usual gathering games for 15 minutes or so, and then begin your usual warm-up. Give them bits and pieces of information about the game rather than all at once.

Etiquette Issues

One of the most important things you should do before game day is to set some team rules. Rather than issuing the rules to your players, have them establish what they—and you—agree are appropriate rules for behavior during the game, including coming on and off the field and etiquette toward other players, their own teammates, and the referees. The more you involve your players, the more they're likely to respect the rules that they've made.

Regarding Referees

Your players are going to look to you as an example, especially in regard to how you treat and respond to referees. If you are screaming at the ref, it won't be long before they are, too. There are going to be good decisions and bad decisions made by the officials, but it is important to respect the calls that are made on the field with good grace. You can certainly talk about them later, but when you are playing a game, the referee should be acknowledged and respected as the sole authority.

Regarding Teammates

You will inevitably have a mix of strong and weak players on your team. It is important that your players respect and appreciate their teammates, regardless of ability. Players should never, under any circumstances, criticize other players. If a player makes a mistake in practice or in a game, have your players encourage her and show support. Never allow a critical remark from a player to another player or to a referee to go without a response. Take that player out of the game at the next out-of-bounds ball, whether it's your best player or your worst. If the remark is made by a player on the sidelines, pull her aside and speak to her. A gentle reminder is all that's needed, but you need to show immediately that team rules must be followed, and that being part of a team means playing in the right spirit with one another and the officials.

Regarding the Opposition

Coaches will often build up the opposing team as a dreaded enemy to be conquered, rather than as a team of kids with the same goals as your own. It's important to establish within your team how you will respond to the other team and how your players will treat them. My philosophy has always been to tell my players, "We don't have to worry about the opposition, but we do need to thank them at the end of the game for giving us the opportunity to play against someone."

You may find that your opposition is waging a hate campaign against your team. The easy way is to react exactly the same way back—but don't

When Players Misbehave

Despite your best efforts, you may have a player who misbehaves on the field. Whether it is mouthing off to the ref, criticizing a teammate or opponent, or throwing a tantrum, you need to take the player off the field immediately. Sometimes you'll have the time to deal with the problem right then and there, which is ideal. Take the player aside and address him about the behavior privately. If there are a lot of things happening and the game is raging, the next best thing is to sit the player down with the team and deal with it later. This helps the whole team stay focused on the game rather than on the player. If the tantrum is serious, you should keep that player out for the rest of the game. This seems like a very long time to players and will send a message about how serious you are about good sportsmanlike behavior. Give the player a day or two to think about his behavior, and then address him privately. Ask the player to tell you what happened and give him a chance to explain himself. Reiterate the rules that the players have established for team behavior, and talk about what was inappropriate about this player's behavior in this particular case. Once you feel you have the issue settled privately with the player, you may consider bringing it up with the team. Let the other players know that this incident is a good lesson about what rules they have established for themselves and how everyone on the team needs to stick to them.

When Parents Misbehave

I was at a U-12 tournament many years ago in which a team from Massachusetts was playing a team from Rhode Island. Tempers flared, and before long parents were shouting and screaming at the referee. I was the referee, but what the parents didn't know was that I was also running the tournament. It wasn't long, of course, until the kids were joining in the yelling. They were just following the example set by the parents. One team won the game, and they suddenly realized that I was also running the tournament and handing over the prize at the end. It was quite interesting because once they realized who I was and my background in the game, they were able to listen to me. I politely but firmly pointed out how much the behavior of both the coaches and the parents affected the kids, and how the adults should set a better example.

do it. Learning that people won't always treat them well but that they should respond to poor behavior with dignity is a good life lesson for your players, and I have found that this approach usually baffles teams that play with poor sportsmanship, giving my own team strength. It also reinforces in your players what playing as a team is all about and gives them a lesson in sportsmanship. This is not always an easy task, because winning is hugely important to kids. It is one of the most important things that's happening to them when they're out there. But it can't become the most important thing for the parent coach or for the coach. It is essential to keep this in mind during the game.

On the Bench

Players on the sidelines are usually eagerly waiting their opportunity to be out on the field, so you shouldn't have any trouble with their behavior. To be honest, I have never experienced a problem with kids waiting to sub in. If they are not closely watching the game, then they are not interested in playing, and obviously it would not be worthwhile to put them into the game. I would explain to these kids that they risk not playing at all.

Game Basics

Although I firmly believe that the key to good soccer is to let the kids play because the game will take care of itself, there are a few times in a soccer match when very specific plays must be accomplished for the game to proceed.

Throw-Ins

When the ball goes out of bounds on the sidelines (or touchlines), a player must make a throw-in to put the ball back into play. The key point to remember about a throw in is that both of the player's feet must stay on the ground behind the sideline as she throws the ball back into play. I like to tell my players to pretend their back foot is an anchor that cannot lift off the ground. I tell them to drag their anchor behind them as they throw the ball in. Remember that players must throw in the ball *straight* over their heads (not to the side or over their shoulders) with both hands on either side of the ball. After throwing in the ball, the player rejoins the action of the game.

Kickoffs

At the beginning of each period and after every goal has been scored, the ball is brought back to the middle of the field to start play. One player from the attacking team runs up to the ball and begins play by "kicking off" the ball onto the opponents' half of the field. Remember that the player who kicked off may not touch the ball again until someone else has touched it. Rules vary from league to league, but generally the ball must roll forward one complete rotation before another team member may touch it. You can have your players develop a number of kickoff plays, such as kicking it back to a halfback or down the wing to a breaking player. Let your players name these plays so they'll remember them.

Corner Kicks

When a member of the defending team plays the ball out of bounds over their own end line, the attacking team is given a chance to kick the ball from the corner of the end and sidelines of the side it went out. If you are not playing a full-field game, the size of the field is usually small enough that the player who takes the corner kick will have the leg strength to get the ball somewhere near the center of the opposing team's goal.

Younger players playing full-field soccer may find it easier to make a few short passes to the goal starting from the corner.

If you're playing on a full-size field, then most players under the age of 12 will have a difficult time kicking the ball near the center of the opposition's goal. One way around this is to have the person taking the corner kick make a short pass to another player on the team who can then make another short pass in front of the goal (see Corner Kick diagram, page 79).

Penalty Kicks

I'm no fan of penalty kicks for young players, because I think it's a hard way to win or lose a game. However, it is important for a coach and the players to know what to do when a penalty kick is called. When defending players commit a foul—usually tripping, pushing, or handling the ball within their own goal area—a player from the opposing team will take a penalty kick from the penalty line, which is 12 yards from the goal, unless otherwise directed by league rules. The goalie stands on the goal line and is not allowed to move his feet until the kicker has moved to kick the ball. As soon as the kicker moves, the goalie can, too.

All the other players on the field stand behind the kicker in back of the penalty area and cannot move toward the ball until the kicker touches it.

Free Kicks

When defending players commit a foul anywhere on the field other than their own goal area, a player from the opposing team will take a free kick toward the goal. Defending players must stand ten yards away from the ball as the player kicks it.

There are two types of free kicks called, depending on the violation, *direct free kicks* and *indirect free kicks*. In a direct free kick, the ball does not need to touch another player before going into the goal. In an indirect free kick, the ball must touch another player before going into the goal.

Make sure you review a dummy game in practice so the team will have a good idea how throw-ins, corner kicks, etc., work. Just spend some time at the end of practice in a mock full game and make sure the players have a good feeling for what will happen. Perhaps an ideal way to prepare is to have a noncount scrimmage with another local team, or perhaps a team from the same club that is a year older. During this scrimmage all the rules and procedures can be gone over while the kids are playing and having fun.

Running the Game

Warm-Up: Keep It Familiar

The most important thing to remember during the warm-up is to make sure you don't have the kids do anything that they haven't done at practice. It's all got to be familiar so that they feel comfortable and find it easy to succeed. Make sure that the drills they do in pairs keep them moving, are pretty easy to accomplish, but also warm them up.

Bring your players out onto the field to warm up as a team. Start them off in pairs, standing about a yard apart and passing a ball between them. The partners should be evenly spaced over the field. After a few moments have them stop passing and leave the balls where they were playing. All the balls will be spaced over the field and will act as a network— players can start doing an exercise at one ball; when they hit the next ball, they alternate with another exercise. For example, you can have them do side-steps with the left leg leading, move to the next ball, and then go side-stepping with the right leg leading. At the next ball, they go back to left leg leading, then right leg leading. You can change the exercise as many times as you want. The important thing is to keep it fun and familiar—it will get your players running gently, moving as a team, and it's easy. When you think they've had enough, have them go back to gently passing the ball between pairs.

It's also a good idea to have your players start playing small games of "keep away," where four players keep the ball away from three without trying to score goals. Every so often during the game of keep away, you should stop the action, have players stretch a bit, and give bits of information about the game, such as which half of the field you'll start on or who will be going into the game first. Keep this information simple, and give it to your players in small doses so they don't get overwhelmed and can remember it.

The goalkeeper will also need to warm up, and it usually is most effective to have an assistant coach take a few players at a time to knock practice shots at the goalkeeper. Avoid having your players stand in lines— keep them moving and passing.

Finish the warm-up, if you can, about 7 minutes before kickoff time and bring your players in around you to get ready for the kickoff.

Substitutions

You should determine your policies for substituting players well before the first game. If league rules require that every player should have equal time, you will need to work out a plan so that you don't have all of your weak players or all of your strong players on at any given time. If your league doesn't have an equal substitution policy, you will need to make a substitute plan that gets everybody on the field through the whole season as often as they can. Obviously in difficult games you will want to try to keep your stronger players in for as long as possible and substitute your weaker players in as often as you can. When you are the stronger team in a game, put your weaker players in for as long as possible and substitute your stronger players in and out. If you are an average team in your league, this should make it so that your strong and weak players are getting approximately equal playing time throughout the season.

Make sure your players know the substitution plan before game time so that they know the roles they will play in the game. You don't need to set up a plan in stone for the whole season, and you can certainly change this plan, but it is important to establish a solid substitution plan early on.

Wee Mike

Kids love stories, and I always have stories to tell players to illustrate a point—stories about myself or a friend or just someone I have heard about. The story of "Wee Mike" is one I often tell when a kid hasn't obtained something he wanted and worked hard for. Perhaps he's on the bench when he wanted to be a starter. Perhaps he didn't get as much playing time as he wanted. In any case, I tell him this story. I played rugby in high school because that was the only team sport offered in the fall and winter quarters. (I played rugby on Saturday morning for the school and then soccer the same afternoon for my club soccer team.) Mike Hunter was always a second-team player when we were in grades 8 to 11. By grade 12, I was beginning to have some success in soccer, so I decided to drop rugby and concentrate my efforts— I was passionate about soccer, so it was an easy choice. With my departure from rugby, Mike came in and took over my position on the first team. At last, in grade 12, he had made the A-team. And history records that Wee Mike became *Big Mike*, who went on as an adult to represent Scotland in international rugby competition. He was the only player from that group to have such success at the sport, yet it took him until his final year in high school even to make the first team.

When you are substituting one player for another on the field, make sure that they know where they are going, who they're going to replace, and what position they are going to play. Tell them this well before they go out on the field, and let them watch their designated player for a few minutes before going in to sub. This will help you avoid having to shout at all of your players to sort out who is going on for whom. It is also a good idea to put one or two substitutes on at a time to avoid confusion. Your league rules may determine how many players may be substituted at a time.

When your players are entering or leaving the field, always put a couple of words of information and encouragement in their ear. The player coming off should shake hands with her sub and then come to you so that you can tell her something that she has done well.

Halftime

Don't try to tell your players too much too soon at halftime. Give them some time to talk among themselves, get a drink of water, and settle down. During this time you can go around and talk to players about individual problems they may be having. Then, after about five minutes or so, bring them in and make two or three basic points that they can work on during the next half. Keep it short, simple, and directive—in fact, this is the only time when you should tell them what they have to do, rather than ask them what they think they should do. For example, if the other team has a very strong player who is consistently taking away the ball and scoring, tell your players to make sure they shut that player down.

When Things Go Wrong—Or Right

If the game is going badly for your team and you are getting a bit of a beating, try to set small, realistic goals for the rest of the game. For example, see if your players can stop the other team from scoring, or have them try to beat their first-half score. The point is to give them a challenge that they can work toward for that time period, rather than dwelling on how badly they are being beaten. There will be games when your players will be outmatched, and this is a good way to make what potentially could be a bad situation into one where they can feel good about accomplishing some immediate objectives.

There will also be games when you will be outscoring another team. This is the time to bring in your weaker players and to work on skills within the game. If you are winning by several goals, have your players work on honing their passing before they shoot again. For example, tell them they have to string ten passes together before they can shoot on goal. Make every game a learning experience, whether you win or lose.

Ending the Game

Regardless of whether you win or lose the game, keep your—and your team's—behavior consistent. The first thing you should do after the final whistle is blown is to shake hands with the opposition coach, the referee, and other officials. This sets an important example for your players. They should also shake hands with the other team and thank the referee for his or her help during the game. Make these game-ending actions rituals that take place after every game. It helps emphasize the importance of good sportsmanship and good manners.

After your players have shaken hands with the other team and officials, gather them together and briefly go over the game. It's very important to be positive about their performance, especially if they have been beaten. Single out the players who did something well, and stress the positive aspects of the game. Let your players know that you saw things they can

Substitute at the Right Time

Try to substitute your players after they've done something well, rather than something poorly. If you're about to substitute for a player and then he makes a real mess of something, such as missing a goal or letting in a bad goal, wait to substitute that player. Let him get over it for a little while, let him get back into the game. Wait until he does something positive; then you take him off.

I always remember a game when we were playing against Harvard in my early years at Dartmouth, and I had a substitute all primed to go in for someone. He was warmed up, he knew who he was going in for, and he was excited about playing. Just at that moment the player whom he was to replace missed an open goal. I just came back and told the substitute, "Sit down. We're leaving him in." I didn't take off a player who had messed up; I didn't take him off at that critical time. In fact, to be honest, I left him in for the rest of the game. I put the substitute in for someone else, but I felt it was a key time for the player who missed the goal to know I supported him and wanted him to succeed on the field. It is vital to respect the feelings of your players, especially with young ones. Always try to bring them off the field on a positive note.

A Few Kind Words

When your team wins, don't forget the opposition. A few words of encouragement can go a long way. I remember on my 13th birthday—the very day—losing a game 13-0. I was playing for Sandyhills YMCA against Peel Glen Amateurs in the Glasgow U-16 YMCA league. As you might expect, I was quite unhappy, but at the end of the game a man from the opposing team approached me—it could have been the coach, but I have no idea. He came over and said, "Great game, son! You really hung in and did a great job. Hold your head up." What a difference these few words of encouragement made to me. Goodness, I still remember it today.

improve on right away, and tell them you'll start working on these things at the next practice. You don't need to mention what they can improve; just letting them know that they can immediately get back on track will help take some of the sting out of losing the game.

Conversely, if your team has won the game, you can be more critical of their performance, telling them that you saw a few things that they could improve. Let them know you're proud of their victory, but remind them that they will face tougher challenges ahead—it helps keep them focused on improving their skills.

Taking Stock

About halfway through your season you should stop and take some time to assess just how things are going for both you and your team. Maybe when you started the season you had visions of future World Cup champions emerging from under your wing, or you were worried that when your team got to a game they'd forget not to touch the ball with their hands. You may have found yourself surprised, either way. Taking stock of how the season is going is a good way to judge what you're doing right as a coach, and what you might need to work on so that you and your players can have a better season.

Ask the Important Questions

The best way to take stock of your season is to gather your players and ask them (and yourself) three important questions:

Keep the Parents at a Distance

Parents are likely to be the most loyal—and vocal—supporters of your team. But the last thing you need during a game is to have your players' parents second-guessing your coaching, trying to discipline their children from the sidelines, or consoling them if they've made a mistake. Make it a policy that parents on your team have to cheer from the other side of the field. They can be as vocal in their support of your team as they want without disrupting the cohesiveness of the team itself. This will help keep things just a little more sane during the game.

The New Kid

When a new player joins an established team, it can be an interesting time. A new player will usually be excited and a bit shy and should be helped through this phase. Try to find out the new kid's ability level right away and make sure she is in comfortable situations. Time will sort all this out, but as the coach you should be aware of how a new kid may feel. Make sure the player is a part of things. Pick her for demonstrations that you know she can do. See that she has an early success.

The team may feel a bit wary of the new kid as well. Keep an eye out for whether the other players on the team have accepted the new kid yet, both as a person and as a player. This is something I go through every year at college as the new recruits come in. I recall a recruit by the name of Vladi Stanojevic. I had watched Vladi play during the recruiting phase, and I knew he would be a huge asset to our Dartmouth team. I didn't, however, start him in the opening match. He came off the bench in that game and scored a goal. I did this for the next game, and the next. I did not start him until the fifth game. By then I knew he was accepted, and the other players all wanted him to do well. His success caused no resentment. Watch how players react to one another. This is a very important skill in coaching—and in any job where you are dealing with people. By the way, Vladi is still the all-time record points scorer for Dartmouth men's soccer, and he didn't start until his fifth game.

- Are you having fun?
- Are you learning something?
- Are you applying what you're learning to the games?

Because one of the most important aspects of the sport for your players will be whether they are winning or losing, if your team is regularly winning, then they're going to be pretty happy. On the other hand, if they're the bottom team in the league, you've got a challenge. Either way, you will need to base your assessment of the season on the premise that you started with— to have fun. This means that you need to keep away from judging the success or failure of your season by what you see in the win-loss column.

If the players and you can answer yes to these questions, then you're running a great ship. It doesn't matter if you aren't winning every game or if you won't end up the league champions. It's clear that your players are happy and are learning the game. But what if they—or you—aren't having fun? If you survey your team and get negative responses to these questions, you need to think about the reasons why things aren't going the way you had hoped or imagined they would.

Give Them Some Challenges

One of the most obvious reasons that your players might not be enjoying the season is if they aren't winning. If your team is halfway through the season and they still haven't won a game, you need to sit down and realistically assess whether or not they will win any. You may recognize that they can't. If so, your job is to come up with challenges for them that make training for the games exciting and fun, and that take the sting out of losing every time.

Give your players some concrete goals to work toward for every game, such as challenging them to score two goals in the next game rather than one, or to hold the other team to half as many goals in the next game as they did in the previous one. If you can make working toward the games as much fun and as good a learning experience as possible, you are doing your job and doing it well.

If you look carefully at your team's abilities and feel that they really could win some games but haven't yet, then make that the challenge for the second half of the season. Get them excited and motivated to make the second half of their season better than the first. Give them a challenge: "Can we win one game? Can we win two games? How many games can we win? How can we improve?" Get them involved, give them goals. Make training for that victory fun.

Get Input from Your Players

One of the best ways to assess how the season is going and to determine what is working and what isn't is to *listen to your players*. Children are pretty perceptive, and if you listen through all their bits and pieces, I think you can quite often get good guidance. Listen to them when you ask them questions, but also listen to them when they're talking out on the field. They'll give you clues about whether they're having a good time, whether they're concentrating, whether they're excited to play the game. For example, if they're playing practice games and nobody knows the score, then something isn't right—they aren't concentrating on what they are doing, and they aren't interested in it. Kids are inherently competitive, so if they are in a game where they don't care who's winning or losing, you know you need to make some changes.

Get Input from the Parents

This is also a good time to talk to the parents again and get their input on how the season is going. Now you can make your points in a roundtable discussion and can discuss even the practical issues of a season that may or may not be going well: Are there problems with traveling? Is the carpooling working? Is everybody fine with the setup for the second half of the season? Are there any better ways to do things? Can we improve in what we're doing? The more input you get, the better it is—parents will have opinions at this midway point in the season; they all have feelings about what's been going on. This gives everybody a chance to air their gripes—or compliments. If they don't come forward at this time, then they've got no right to complain.

What Next?

After everyone has given you their input about the first half of the season, make your new aims and objectives for the second half of the season. Look at them realistically—it should be easier to make your assessment now because you've seen the level of the competition, and you know your own team's abilities. Above all, having fun and learning to enjoy the game should remain your primary goals for your players.

Questions and Answers

Q. I have a player who has done very well in practice, but he has decided he doesn't want to play in our first game. What should I do?

A. Keep the player coming to the games, and suggest that he sub in every so often, whenever he feels ready. Keep asking, but don't push. You may also want to talk to the parents about the situation to find out if they know why the player is reluctant to join in.

Q. A parent of one of my players is very concerned that his child didn't have enough playing time in our first game. Our league doesn't have an equal playing time rule, and this kid is not very good. I want to make sure every child gets to play as much as possible—how can I make sure I'm not leaving anyone out?

A. In general, you should keep the playing time of your players as fair as possible. Play your strongest players up the middle, and put your weaker ones on wide areas. Always try to put a balanced team on the field, so that you aren't putting your two strongest or two weakest players on the field at any given time. There may be a game where you have to play strong players, since kids really *do* care about winning, but you need to keep it as balanced and fair as possible. Don't make it obvious that you are putting on weak players just for the sake of playing them. You'll need to address this carefully and work out appropriate substitutions so that the whole team's morale stays high—just as you don't want to disappoint anyone, you also don't want to overwhelm a player, either.

Q. I made it clear that I expected my players to respect the referees and their decisions, but the ref we had at the first game was terrible and clearly didn't know some of the rules of the game. I didn't say anything at the time, but after the game my players had questions about the rules and the official. What do I tell them?

A. Tell your players that referees aren't always good, but that the players have to respect the spirit of the game. Remind them that they do this when they are playing games at practice without a referee. Mention that they know the rules but that they have to accept the referee's decisions. You can tell them that bad calls happen at the highest levels, but that everyone—players, parents, and coaches—needs to accept the ref's decisions.

Q. We won our first game, and after it was over some of my players were whooping and shouting. I was glad they were excited, but how much celebrating after a win is too much?

A. It's good to be happy after a win, but remind players that they need to be careful not to rub it in. It's natural for players to be excited and exuberant, but don't allow chants and whooping. Celebrate the win, shake the other teams' hands, calm down, and respect the other team.

Q. During the game our team completely fell apart, and I panicked. How can I make sure it doesn't happen again?

A. Try to visualize what could happen before the game—think of all the scenarios that could take place, such as being overwhelmed by your opponents. Really, though, what's the worst thing that could happen? You lose the game. Everyone, sooner or later, will lose a game. You need to keep your composure so that your players will, too—and you need to prepare your players for the possibility that they might lose. You and they should both be concentrating on all the things you worked on at practice—and the winning and losing will take care of itself.

Q. Our team lost in a huge way. The kids worked hard and played well, but we were simply outmatched. They are feeling very low—how can I get them back on track and excited again?

A. This is another example of learning a life lesson—you have to let them know that you're all in this together, and there will always be a losing team and a winning team. Stress the positive things your players did during the game. Acknowledge the skills of the other team, and let their skills set the standard you will try to reach next time.

Q. We won our first game by a huge goal margin. I'm proud of the kids, but I want to make sure they don't focus solely on winning. How do I address success?

A Now is a good time to make some critical suggestions to your players—they are more receptive to criticism after a win. Definitely say that they did well, but make concrete suggestions for improvement. You can also do this during a game where your team is way ahead. Rather than running up the score, for example, have your players work on stringing together six passes before they can shoot on goal, or tell them they can only score off a heading shot. The important thing to emphasize is to keep both winning and losing in perspective—it's great that they won, but they will certainly face challenges in the future.

Q. I have several players who have recently become less regular about attending practices. When I've brought it up they say, "Oh, I had something else going on that day," but it's dragging down the rest of the team. What do I do?

A. If you find that your players aren't all coming to practice regularly, you will need to sit down with them and emphasize that when they joined the team at the beginning of the season, it was a promise to many other people that they would come to practice and games and would participate with enthusiasm. People always get excited about new things, but once the glamour phase wears off, they're looking for something else that's new and exciting. It's a very important life lesson for children to learn that when they make a commitment they need to stick to it and honor it. If necessary, talk to their parents and let them know that their children need to stick with the commitment they made this season to come to practice and the games.

Q. My team is terrible—there's no other way to say it. It's unlikely we will win any games this season, and they know it. How can I keep them excited about the rest of the season without being patronizing about the goals we set for ourselves?

A. It is important to set some realistic goals when your team isn't as skilled as the other teams in the league. Most teams will play each other several times during a season. Use your past performance against a particular team as the benchmark to set new goals, such as keeping the score against you lower than it was the last game. You can also strive for different types of goals: for example, rather than worrying about the score, challenge your players to work on their passing or heading. The key is to set realistic goals so that the game remains fun and challenging and not demoralizing.

CHAPTER 8

Dealing with Parents and Gender Issues

Parents are the most enthusiastic supporters of youth sports you'll ever find: they come to games, regardless of the weather, they bake dozens of cookies and drive to faraway towns without a whimper, and they cheer loudly for their kids' teams, no matter how lopsided the score. Parents are such strong supporters of their kids, in fact, that you may find they want to do more than just cheer for their kids: they may want to "help" you coach, too. The best way to deal with potential parent-related problems is to address them before the season starts, in either your parents meeting or through a letter sent home at the beginning of the first practice.

The Role of the Parents

The Golden Rule for Parents: Support the Coach without Actually Coaching

A little soccer knowledge can be a real pain for a coach—there's nothing worse than having a parent who chips away at your authority and coaching skills because they "know a thing or two" about the sport. You need to be perfectly clear from the beginning that their role is to support the team by supporting your decisions at all times. You don't need to pretend to be a soccer guru, and you can certainly let them know that their input is welcome at appropriate times, but it needs to be clear to the parents that the worst thing they can do for their children is to double-coach them by second-guessing you. It's important to point out that every comment, even those that their kids overhear at the dinner table, can have an effect on their children's attitudes.

During practices or games, the best place for the parents is on the other side of the field, where they can be supportive from a distance. Part of the reason for this is team based: it's important that when kids come off the field during a game, they focus on being a part of a team, rather than an individual. If things haven't gone well, they shouldn't be able to come off the field and go to their parents for consolation—they've got to be consoled within the team, with the coach and with each other.

The best thing parents can do for their children is to get them to practices and games on time, always remain positive about what their children do on the field, and reinforce and support your coaching decisions.

Winning Isn't the Only Thing

Like you, the parents of your players need to keep winning and losing in careful perspective—they have to be above caring too much about whether their children win or lose games, since their kids will care so much. Parents also need to be comfortable with the playing time their children get on the field, and should trust you to be fair and substitute players appropriately. There may be games where the policy is free substitution, and inevitably someone's child will have only a minor role in the game. Parents need to use discretion and be supportive of your decisions on the field.

Let the Parents Voice Their Opinions

You don't need a special meeting to get feedback from parents—make it clear that you have an "open door" policy where they are welcome and encouraged to talk with you about how things are going, as long as it is in an appropriate time and place. One great way to get feedback from parents is through social events such as postgame cookouts or picnics. If you give parents the opportunity to tell you what's on their minds in a nonconfrontational environment, you'll pick up some great information about your season and your team.

Get Them Involved

The more you can get parents involved in off-field activities surrounding your team, the better. If you have a soccer parent who is coordinating other administrative duties as team manager, he or she can help organize other off-field activities as well, such as fund-raising, carpooling, or cookouts.

Parents Who Don't See the Funny Side of Life

I still remember an episode brought about by Ralph Ferrigno, my first assistant at Dartmouth, who was running our spring camp. Ralph is an excellent coach for all ages and has a great sense of humor. He loves to play games, and to enforce the dress code he would have a camp inspection every morning. He would line the kids up army style, have them stand at attention, at ease, right turn, and all the rest. It was meant to be fun, and the kids loved the parody of seriousness that Ralph put into the little show. However, one day a parent called my office quite upset and complained about how strictly I was running this camp. "It's like the military!" he declared. I finally convinced him that this was an elaborate joke, part of the make-believe world that we create. It was meant to be a part of the fun, and I encouraged him to come down and observe.

Parents want to be a part of their children's lives, and this is an ideal way to do it.

Addressing Gender Issues

When you're dealing with young kids, my philosophy has always been that the fewer rules in regard to gender issues, the better. Kids in particular have a real way of sorting things out. If I have a coed team and say to a group of players, "OK. Everybody pair up and get a ball," it's very likely that the top two players will be paired up, and if we have a couple of weaker players, there's a good chance they will paired up, too. If we have six girls, we will probably see three sets of partners, with the girls pairing up with one another to do these drills. That just happens—kids don't necessarily take gender into account when they are choosing partners for drills; they will often choose people most like them in ability. Try to let your players sort themselves out, regardless of gender—you will probably find that players of like ability will often match up.

Younger kids often compete against each other across gender up to the sixth or seventh grade. After that, the kids generally take it upon themselves to split up and play boys against boys, and girls against girls. Each situation may be different, but if you just let things happen and don't create an issue at the outset, everyone becomes comfortable with whatever situa-

For younger kids, the fewer rules in regard to gender issues, the better.

tion works out. With the younger kids, try and encourage a variety of group-ings so the boys and girls are actively practicing together. While it makes sense that boys and girls get separated in later years, in my opinion it is not essential. I have a daughter and two sons, all of whom have played soccer. In many ways the better girl players get much more out of playing with boys. Many girls who go on to become outstanding women players played on boys teams. It certainly makes them competitive. Whether the players are male or female, or black, white, or yellow, the principles of playing together as a team and supporting one another should be paramount.

Girls tend to take criticism very personally, and they also want to know the rationale behind a particular drill or skill, whereas most boys I've coached would run through a wall if I told them to and wouldn't question why they were doing it. You won't have to change any drills or your coach-ing philosophy. Just be prepared to offer girls more information and proba-bly a bit more direction. You'll find that the girls are just as competitive as boys, and often much more coachable. It's all in how you bring that com-petitive spirit out in them.

That being said, whereas younger kids often compete against each other across gender up to the sixth or seventh grade, by the teenage years teams should be single gender if possible. Otherwise, boys tend to dominate the play, and the differences in the learning style for girls and boys, as well as their emotional differences, make it a good idea to give them their own teams. Girls and boys are motivated in different ways, so what works with the girls may fail miserably with the boys. Athletics is a natural place for girls to develop confidence and assertive behavior, and by junior high the presence of boys can diminish the experience—maybe not for all girls or in every situation, but certainly for some. By this age, sports should be separate from the boy-girl stuff that will certainly be starting for many kids, making them self-conscious with the opposite gender.

Questions and Answers

Q. I have some parents who keep giving their kids "advice" about their performances after games and practices, but I really disagree with their suggestions. How do I address this?

A. This is a difficult issue, and the best approach to take is to go directly to the parent and privately explain your views. You may find that the parent has something to teach you, so come to the conversation with an open mind. The most important thing to stress when you speak to the parent is that the child shouldn't be getting mixed messages from the parents and coach.

Q. Some parents insist on sitting right behind the bench and making comments during the game about the other team and the refereeing.

I made it clear during the parents meeting that I wanted them on the other side of the field, but a few just don't seem to care. I know they are trying to be supportive to the kids and the team, but I don't like it. What's a diplomatic solution here?

A. This is a good job for the parent manager—it's a good idea not to get involved in this issue yourself. Your primary concern should be coaching the kids, not babysitting the parents.

Q. I am worried that some of the parents aren't at all interested in what their kids are doing, and that their children might be feeling bad about it. How can I encourage these parents to be more supportive and to participate more in their kids' activities?

A. In my experience, most kids don't really notice if their parents are involved or not—they are too busy having fun. Kids need rides to practices and to games, and that's really all the involvement parents absolutely need to have. If the kids enjoy what they are doing, they won't be looking around for their parents—it's not the reason they are playing. Usually it's the adults who get more caught up in worrying about parent interest than the kids. However, if your players bring it up, you can mention it to the parents to give them a wake-up call.

Q. I have a parent who constantly questions my judgment about how much time each team member plays. She feels that her child, who is quite good, is not playing enough. I have explained that it is important for every team member to play, regardless of ability. We simply don't see eye-to-eye on this, and the parent cannot accept my explanation.

A. The early team meeting is critical for explaining your policy on substitution: discuss the policy of subbing with the parents and make sure you come to an agreement about how you will do it. That way, if it becomes a problem during the season, you can remind the parents that they were in agreement about the substitution policy and how your rules are the rules of the team. If for some reason the parents can't deal with that, they are free to take their child to another team.

Q. I have a parent who is incredibly critical of his child. He has a negative way of shouting orders to this child when she's playing and then instructs her when she's on the bench about how she should have done something differently. How can I diplomatically ask the parent to back off and adopt a more positive attitude?

A. This is one reason why the preseason meeting is so important. During that meeting, you will have stressed that only positive comments should be made by both players and their parents, and there should be no parents sitting behind the bench. If for some reason parents can't remember or heed these rules, use your parent manager to talk to that person. If it continues to be a real problem, you will have to talk to the parent yourself, but this is another example of where you shouldn't have to be dealing with parent behavior.

Q. I have a team of both boys and girls. In the drills the girls always tend to partner with girls, and the boys with boys rather than by equal skill level. Should I let them do this, or pair them by skill level regardless of gender?

A. You can either select partners for skill drills or positions, or you can let them choose partners themselves. In my experience, girls are more inclined to go with friends, regardless of ability, while boys will pair up based on the level of competition they can get, regardless of friendship. If your players are happy with the way they are paired up, let them do it. Players tend to sort these things out well among themselves. However, if players aren't learning the skills or are having trouble because their skill levels are uneven, give them some time to try it together and then mix up the pairings to give everyone a new partner. This will allow your players some autonomy but will also solve uneven skill problems if they arise. In drills where strong players should be paired off with players of similar ability, such as One-on-One Soccer, you may want to assign partners.

Q. My team has only one girl on it. She seems very comfortable and confident with the boys, but some of the boys are not comfortable with her. What should I do?

A. These things only become problems when you make them so. You can discuss this situation privately with the boys who are having trouble adjusting to the girl, but if she can play well, they'll accept her. If the sole girl on a team is a noticeably weaker player, she could become uncomfortable. Find something that she does well and praise her for it. Make sure that the boys are aware of her contributions. As a coach, you should reinforce the principle that everyone is an equal part of the team, regardless of gender, speed, skill level, or anything else. The more you stress the importance of valuing each individual on the team, the more your team will accept and appreciate it.

Q. The boys on my team always hog the ball. They consistently pass only to other boys, ignoring the girls. What should I do?

A. Here are several ideas:

1. Stage a two-on-two game in practice, each team with a boy and a girl. If there are more boys, put two weaker boys together.

2. Practice and implement into games specifically designed plays in which boys and girls have different roles and must pass to each other. Call out these plays in the game if boys aren't passing to girls.

3. Take the boy or boys aside privately and speak to them individually about the matter, emphasizing the sense of "team." They should understand what is involved in being a member of the team and earning playing time on the team—namely, passing to all available teammates.

Q. Some of the strategies I use with the girls work really well, but the boys don't seem to respond.

A. You need to expect that some kids will not respond to certain methods or drills, and thus you need to teach in a variety of ways. You will encounter such a problem with a team of all boys or all girls as well, and you need to alter drills or concepts in order to try and reach each player. Consequently, plan relatively short and frequently changing drills.

CHAPTER 9

Games and Drills

Warm-Up

Stuck in the Mud   1

This very simple game not only gives the kids a chance to get moving but also makes them think ahead: how do they "unstick" their teammates without getting caught themselves?

Give three kids pinnies and have them run around the soccer field trying to tag the other players. When they tag someone, perhaps on the top of the head or on the back, the person who has been tagged is frozen—he is stuck in the mud. The only way he can get free is for one of his teammates to crawl through his legs and release him. Give the three taggers a minute to see how many players they can get stuck in the mud.

Pairs Chasing   2

Divide your players into pairs and have the partners connect themselves to one another. They can link up with one arm on each other's shoulder so that they form a little bridge and can only take side steps. You can have them link arms going forward, or they can link arms so that one partner is facing forward and the other partner is facing backward, which makes it a little bit more complicated to move. One team is "it" and chases the other teams of two. Once a team has been tagged, the partners have to freeze and hold hands, but they can be freed if another pair comes under the bridge that they're making with their hands. A variation on the game is for you to give the teams that are caught a little forfeit, such as three push-ups, three knees to the chest, or something else fun, and then the partners are released.

Caterpillar   3

Have your players divide into groups or chains of three, consisting of a lead person, a middle person holding onto the shoulders of the person in front of her, and an end person holding onto the shoulders of the middle person. You can do this with up to four or five people in a caterpillar chain. This is a tagging game, with each caterpillar trying to tag the last person in another caterpillar chain, while at the same time trying to avoid being tagged. It's a fast-moving game that forces players to coordinate their movements as a team and to think quickly.

Odd Man Out 4

This is also a tagging game. Three people link arms, with the two on the outside facing one direction, and the middle person facing the opposite direction. Teams try to tag each other while trying to avoid being tagged. The setup of the players makes it difficult to run and requires players to concentrate on moving, reacting to other teams, and thinking on their feet.

Triangle Tag 5

The aim of this game is to protect the person in the middle of the triangle. Players form groups of three and link arms, with the middle kid wearing a pinny. The tagger tries to touch the player in the pinny while the other two players in the triangle try to protect him. This game helps the players learn to move and to avoid defenders.

Snake Tag 6

In another variation of tag, three players form a line or chain. The first person has her arms free. Behind her is the second person, who holds onto the waist or shoulders of the first player. The third player wears a pinny and holds onto the waist or shoulders of the second player. The person who is "it" tries to tag the third player, while the other two attempt to protect her.

Relays 7

These relays take little technical ability, but a good bit of teamwork and cooperation and a lot of energy are required. Leave the players on their teams from the gathering activity (or divide them into more evenly balanced teams). Players stand in lines and run relay races out to a marker (perhaps a cone) and back. Have them start with running, hopping, skipping, and so on. Then give each team a ball. The first person on each team runs out to the marker and back, holding the ball. His other team members all stand close together in a line with their feet spread wide apart. The first runner rolls the ball through the tunnel formed by their legs. The person at the end of the tunnel catches the ball, runs out to the marker and back, and rolls the ball back through the tunnel of legs. The relay continues until everyone on the team runs to the marker and rolls the ball through the tunnel of legs. Then everyone sits down. You can run the relay with players passing over the other players, passing through their legs, or performing whatever other variations you or your players think of.

Chain Tag   8

This is a simple and effective warm-up that helps teach cooperation and teamwork. Mark off a small area of the field, no larger than 20 by 20 yards. Start off with one person being the chaser, with the whole team running within a confined area. The first person who is tagged joins the chaser to form a chain, and the two tag other players. As more players are tagged, they join the chain. Keep the game going until your time is up (you determine the time limits), or until there is only one person left outside the chain. This person is the winner.

Numbers Warm-Up   9

This warm-up game may be played with or without a ball.

Without a ball: Give each warm-up exercise a number. Number 1 could be side steps, number 2 butt kicks, number 3 knees up, and so on. Call out the various numbers, and players must perform the exercises. Start with a couple of numbers and then add on exercises as the squad catches on. Explain that, similar to the game of Simon Says, the word *number* needs to be said; if *number* is left out, then the players should ignore the command. As you say the numbers, start leaving out the word *number* every so often. Anyone who does the exercise anyway has to do a forfeit, such as three knees to chest, and then catches up with the group. Add another degree of difficulty by adding "turn" and "change" commands to the drill. When you shout, "Turn," players do a complete 360-degree turn and keep on running; when you shout, "Change," they do a 180-degree turn and go off in the reverse direction. You can even make this more difficult by using body language to trap players into doing the wrong action. All of this is just a fun way to get the kids listening and concentrating.

With a ball: In a variation of the basic game, each dribbling move is given a number. Number 1 could be stop and start, number 2 a spin-in (see Turns and Spins in the next section). When you call out a number, players have to perform that dribbling move. This is similar to giving each move a player's name. The game helps the players learn to listen and concentrate.

Ball Handling

Change Game   10

This drill helps your players become comfortable running with a ball between their feet. The drill will also keep your players listening for your instructions and working on disciplined movement, as well as being aware of other players on the field. Have your players out on the field dribbling. When you shout, "Change!" everyone has to stop their balls, leave them, and find another unattended ball. The last person to locate another ball has to do a forfeit.

Finger Game   11

This game teaches your players to dribble with their heads up. Spread your players out around the field, and have them work their way around the field dribbling. As they practice their ball control, put your hand in the air and hold up one, two, or three fingers at a time. The first person to identify how many fingers you are holding up gets a point.

Numbers Game #1   12

This drill helps players work on ball control, dribbling skills, and thinking and reacting to what's going on around them. Explain to your players that you will call out a number, and each number has a skill they must do. The skills rhyme with the number, and for younger players, you can have them call out the skill as they do it.

Number 1: on your bum. Players stop, hold the ball, and sit on the ground.
Number 2: under your shoe. Players stop the ball with the soles of their shoes.
Number 3: under your knee. Players stop the ball and kneel on the ground.
Number 4: hit the floor. Players stop dribbling, hit the ground with both hands, and then resume dribbling.
Number 5: do a jive. Players stop and run around the ball one time.
Number 6: do some tricks. Players do any dribbling move.
Number 7: up to heaven. Players toss up the ball and head it once.

Keep going if you can.

Truck and Trailer Game   13

Although it sounds simple, this drill can be quite difficult to accomplish well. The goal is for your players to hone their ball-control skills so that they can easily dribble in pursuit of a player directly in front of them without losing control of their own ball.

Divide your players into pairs, with one player standing behind the other. The lead player (the "truck") starts dribbling, and the following player (the "trailer") has to dribble her ball close behind, never getting more than a few steps behind the truck. At your whistle, have the partners stop and see how close the trailer is to the truck. Any team more than a yard or two apart should do a forfeit.

Spaceman   14

Arrange your players throughout a defined space on the field, say a 30-by-30-yard square, and have them start dribbling. Tell them that they are spacemen who must be aware of the space they are taking up and that as a team they have to cover all of the allotted space. Remind them throughout the drill by asking them, "Are you watching your space?" This will help keep their heads up. When you shout, "Stop," the whole area your team is in should be fairly evenly covered by the players. If they are all spaced out, then you lose and have to do a forfeit. If they are bunched up in areas, with large areas of the square bare, they need to pay a forfeit. You don't need to spend much time explaining the concept of space before beginning this drill: players will intuitively understand the concept by doing it them-selves through the discovery method (see the Discovery Method sidebar on page 16). You can periodically give them some little pointers as they drib-ble. Get your players moving, and then every so often yell, Freeze!" When they freeze, ask, "Are we covering all the space within this 30-by-30-yard box? and "Are we moving all the time?" They will learn that when one kid moves out of a space, someone else must move into that space. The whole drill is just a big continuous movement, with everyone keeping their eyes up and concentrating on filling the space. Since they're moving all the time, there are always going to be spaces being created, so there are always spaces needing to be filled. This drill can be a lot of fun.

Black Hole 15

This is a variation on Spaceman. Set up a smaller square within the 30-by-30-yard area that is approximately 15 by 15 yards. As the players play Spaceman in the entire 30-by-30-yard area, you yell, "Black Hole." They immediately all move into the smaller space, where they must continue to dribble their balls without touching each other. When you announce, "Spaceman," players move back out into the larger field. Switch between the two playing areas several times. This game gives players a sense of main-taining space in both large areas and close quarters.

Turns and Spins 16

The next skill to add in is a *basic turn*, which is very similar to a stop. The player puts the sole of his foot on the ball and slows it down. Then he turns and goes the other way. It seems—and is—very easy, and most of the kids will pick it up pretty quickly. After they have worked on basic turns, intro-duce spin-outs and spin-ins. A *spin-out* is a turn in which the player spins the ball on the outside of his foot. A *spin-in* is a turn using the inside of the foot. These spins help your players learn to make tight turns. Incorporate these "speedboat turns" into the game of Change.

This is an easy drill that will help your players hone their turning skills. It will also keep them aware of your signal and other players on the field. Spread your players out over the field and have them begin dribbling the ball. Call out the direction of the turn or spin you want them to make: "Turn with the outside foot," "Inside foot," "Sole turn." You can vary the speed of your commands or make it more competitive by making the last player to complete a turn do a forfeit.

GAMES AND DRILLS

Sharks and Minnows   17

This game is great for working on ball-handling skills and for heads-up soccer. You'll also find that this will be many kids' favorite game. Mark off an area on the field as the pond. Choose a couple of players to be sharks—they won't have balls, but they are on the prowl for someone else's ball. All the other players are minnows dribbling around the pond. The sharks must try to take someone else's ball away or kick that person's ball out of the pond. If they succeed, then they become a minnow, and the person whose ball was kicked out becomes the shark.

A variation of Sharks and Minnows is to have two areas: one pond where all the minnows are swimming around with their balls and another pond area where they need to go before 10 or 15 seconds are up (longer than that, and the game becomes too slow). Between the two ponds are the rapids, where the shark (in this case probably you or an assistant) is waiting. If the shark kicks a minnow's ball away as the minnow swims through the rapids, the minnow must join the shark. Eventually you'll end up with almost everyone being sharks and perhaps just one minnow trying to swim between the ponds with his ball. The two-pond game is great because the kids have to keep their heads up to keep an eye on the shark, and they have to determine how and when to sneak by the shark through the rapids.

King of the Ring   18

This is a great game for learning the fundamentals of soccer because it incorporates ball-handling skills and the concept of being aware of defenders and action on the field.

Make a square or ring of cones, the size of which will depend on your squad size. Each player has a ball to dribble and must stay within the ring. The point of the game is for the players to keep control of their balls while trying to kick someone else's ball out of the ring. The balls are never allowed to be stationary, so players can't leave their balls to go after someone else's ball. If a ball does stop moving, this is the same as having it knocked out of the ring. You might set the rules that when a ball is stopped or kicked out, that player is out. The game continues until there is only one player left.

You can also play the game with "lives," where players get three lives. Each time their ball is knocked out or stops, they lose a life until they've used up their three lives. Or you might say that when a ball is stopped or knocked out, that player has to do a forfeit, such as three push-ups and six sit-ups, and then the player can join back in the game. At the end of the game you can count up how many players had to do one forfeit, how many had to do two forfeits, and so on. This is a great game for teaching the fundamentals of soccer because it incorporates ball-handling skills and the concept of always being aware of what's going around you.

One-on-One Soccer   19

As your players become more comfortable moving the ball with their heads up, have them play short one-on-one games. These intense games are some of the best training your players will do.

First, divide the team into pairs and have one player from each pair place her ball several yards away. This ball will be the goal.

Then, the two players play one-on-one, each trying to control the ball in play. Whichever player manages to hit the "goal" ball with the ball in play wins a point.

One-on-one games are very demanding and tiring, especially for younger players. Make sure you stop these games often to make plenty of coaching points—it will give players a rest and will give you an opportunity to explain, for instance, how to defend the ball by keeping it on the outside foot and changing speed and direction. Or you might pick out a couple of kids who are performing well and have them demonstrate a good change of direction or a particularly good move while the rest of the group takes a breather.

One of the nicest aspects of one-on-one games is that although they are simple in design, they help players learn and practice important fundamental skills while having fun. Most young players love the competitive aspect of such games.

Sometimes when you're doing one-on-one games it's good to put your players in groups of four so you always have two people resting and two people going. The easiest way to do this is to divide the large field into minifields, about 15 yards in length by 10 yards wide, with two little goals at either side, approximately a yard or two yards apart. The two resting players could sit and watch the two other players, or they could be neutral players on the sidelines, where they're allowed one touch. That's quite a good way to keep them occupied, interested, and involved while they're basically resting. Switch players often.

World Cup Games   20

One of the fun ways to develop a good dribbling game is to divide your players into small groups of four to play World Cup. Divide the large field into minifields, about 15 yards in length by 10 yards wide. One player becomes the goalkeeper, and each of the other three players assumes a country's name and becomes that country's World Cup soccer team. The goalkeeper kicks the ball out, and the other three players compete with one another to see who can get the ball and score goals on the goalkeeper. The first country to score three goals wins the World Cup.

A variation of World Cup Games that works well with larger groups of players (five or six players per group) is to create elimination rounds. The first person to score automatically goes into the next round of the World Cup. Play continues until there is only one player who hasn't scored. This player is eliminated, and the others go on to the next round. One player continues to be eliminated each round until eventually there is one World Cup champion. This form of World Cup is a good game for players to do on their own rather than at practice, since the kids who get eliminated early are sitting out for most of the game. Or you could have a game ready for them to play while the World Cup rounds continue.

One-on-One Ladder   21

In the One-on-One Ladder many one-on-one games take place simultaneously. Create as many minifields as there are pairs of players. Number the pairs—these will be your divisions. As the partners play one-on-one, they keep score of the goals they make. When you call time, the winners of each division stay where they are, and the loser moves to the next lower division (except for the last division, where the winner goes up, and the loser goes down). The appeal of the One-on-One Ladder is that the games are short and intense, and there are immediate winners and losers. Let the games go for maybe a minute, a minute and a half, and then you change them over. There's always movement because as players win and lose, they move on to play other players.

Team Tag   22

Divide your players into three teams, and give each team a different colored pinny (if available). Each player has a ball to dribble. While they're dribbling, you shout out where and when they should turn, similar to the Turns and Spins game. Every so often you shout out "Yellow's tag!" (or whatever color). The yellow team then becomes the chasers, who chase the other two teams while everyone remains dribbling. Every time a player on one of the other two teams is tagged, she must stop and hold her ball above her head and stand with her legs wide apart. The only way she can be released from the tagged position is if one of her own team members dribbles a ball through her legs. The game continues until all of the members of one team get tagged.

Passing and Receiving

Numbers Game #2   23

This game helps players keep their heads up when they are preparing to pass. Divide your players into pairs and have them pass back and forth, gently, with their partners. The receiver should raise his hand and put up one to five fingers. Before the passer passes the ball to the receiver, he has to shout out the number of fingers the receiver is holding up.

Soccer Marbles   24

This game will help your players work on their passing accuracy. Divide your players into partners. Each partner will have a ball. Each player's soccer ball is a marble: one player tries to hit her partner's marble to win points. The first to reach five points wins, and the other player has to do an easy forfeit.

Divide your team into partners and start your players approximately six yards apart within a certain boundary—closer or farther depending on their skill level. Stress that players are trying to go for accuracy, so they should work on soft passing with no wet fish. One player goes first and continues playing until he misses. Then it's the next player's turn. Whoever makes it to five points first wins.

Pass and Receive, Head Up   25

The proper way to receive a ball is with both the foot and the head coming up. If a player can do that in one touch, then it means that her head comes up immediately after reception. If the player needs to take another touch to set the ball up, then her head has to go down again. If she needs two touches to set it up, her head has to go down twice, and so on. The more times her heads goes down, the less time her head is up to see what the other players are doing and to make a decision. Your goal is to teach your players "heads-up soccer."

Start your players off in pairs. Each partner receives the ball in front of him with one touch of the foot and passes it back with the second touch. One-touch passing will get your players to concentrate both on passing the ball and on receiving it. Remind your players that when they make an inside-of-the-foot pass, the standing foot should come alongside the ball and should come in behind the ball, not across it.

Triangle Game   26

This game helps players learn to pass and receive the ball properly. Take three cones (or balls or pinnies) and create a triangle that is about two or three yards long on each side. Divide your players into teams of two-on-two and have them take cones and make the same triangles out around the field. One pair in each foursome begins the game.

The person with the ball has to pass it through the cone triangle and out the other side without touching any of the cones. Her partner has to receive the ball and play it through a different side of the triangle back to the first player. The ball cannot be played back through the same side twice in a row. Every time a player passes it successfully through the triangle, that counts as one point. The pair in each foursome that isn't playing keeps track of the score, and as soon as the first pair either hits a cone or passes the ball back through the same side, they stop playing and let the counters play. The winner at the end is the pair with the highest score.

Triangle Game Progression   27

This variation of the Triangle Game will help your players work on receiving the ball on different surfaces of their bodies. The partners play the game the same way as before, but this time they are to use the outside or inside of the foot and then take the ball across the body to the other foot. If the player receives with the right foot, for example, he moves the ball over to the opposite side and makes his return pass with his left foot. The next variation could be receiving the ball on the inside foot and pushing it to the outside of the body. A further variation might be using the outside of the foot to set the ball up. Always bring these progressions back to the triangle passing and receiving game.

Passing Contest   28

Players pair up and begin the Passing Contest by passing the ball softly back and forth to each other. Once they have had a bit of a warm-up, time their passing for one minute and have them count their passes during this time period. As you time, walk around and take points off for bad form, such as "wet fish" passing. The high score wins, with all the other pairs doing two knees to the chest for a forfeit.

You can add complexity to this drill by stipulating that players alternate feet when they pass or alternate passing with the inside and outside of their feet. Or, you could have one player stop the ball with the sole of her foot and then have her partner come and touch her hand to the ball, then run back to her original position to get ready for the pass before resuming the game.

Multigoal Game   29

This drill gets players working on passing and coordinating with a partner for heads-up dribbling, plus they must be aware of what goes on everywhere on the field. This is fun and challenging, and your players will like the competitive aspect of it.

Divide your players into pairs. Set up a series of small goals, approximately one or two yards apart, throughout the 30-by-30-yard practice area, making sure you have as many goals as there are pairs. Give your pairs 30 seconds to see how many goals they can pass through in that time. The pair that passes through the fewest number of goals in 30 seconds has to pay a forfeit. They cannot go to a goal they have already played or to a goal at which another pair is playing; they have to look for a goal that's empty. Not only are your players passing and coordinating with their partners, but they also have their heads up, they're looking for goals that aren't being used, and they have to remember which goals they have already gone through. This is fun and challenging, and your players will like the competitive aspect of it.

Team Relays   30

Divide your players into even teams. Set up alternating cones so that the practice field looks like a slalom course. Your players will have to pass to each other through the gates and work their way up and back down the slalom course. The team with the most clean passes in the shortest amount of time wins. This drill works equally well with dribbling or with a combination of passing and dribbling. It's a great drill to get players focusing on teamwork, passing, and dribbling skills in combination.

Team Cricket   31

This is another drill that combines dribbling and passing. Divide your players into two teams. One team will be a relay team dribbling through a series of cones arranged in a circle. The length of the cricket "inning" will be as long as it takes for the last person on the circular series to make it through the cones. While one team is doing this, the other team will be inside the circular cones doing a passing relay through an alternating slalom course, trying to see how many passes they can get through. When the inning is over, the teams add up their passes and switch positions. After an even number of innings, a winner is determined by the highest score.

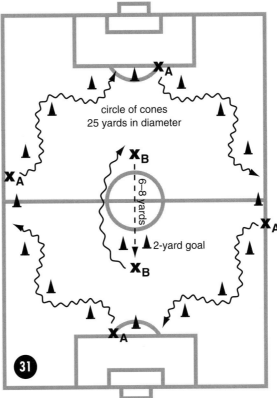

circle of cones
25 yards in diameter

6–8 yards

2-yard goal

Soccer cricket. Members of team A dribble through a circular series of cones while members of team B work on a passing relay. When both teams have finished their respective challenges, they switch.

Piggy in the Middle   32

This is a more competitive, gamelike drill that incorporates the use of defenders trying to steal passes. Set up a 20-by-20-yard playing area, and divide your players into groups of four, with one person in the middle and the three others trying to pass the ball to one another. The object of the game is to keep the ball away from the person in the middle by passing. If the player in the middle touches the ball or the ball goes out of the grid, then the person who last played it becomes the new piggy in the middle.

It is best to limit the number of players in this game to three versus one because it forms a triangle for passing. The person with the ball needs the two people supporting, and when the ball gets played to one of the supporting players, then everyone has to move again to keep the triangle with good supporting options. All three players need to put themselves in positions where they can see the whole field. This is an important concept for later use, and if players can learn this at an early age, it will be helpful to their development.

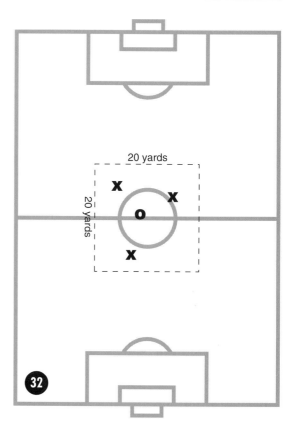

20 yards

20 yards

32

In Piggy in the Middle, if a defender (O) kicks the ball outside the grid, the last player (X) to touch the ball becomes the new "piggy in the middle."

Four-on-Two Keep Away   33

When your players have become comfortable with the three-on-one Piggy in the Middle game, you can make the game more complicated by adding more players. Another version is to divide your players into pairs and to create a 20-by-40-yard grid on the field for each group of three pairs. Two pairs of players must now keep the ball away from the interior pair. As soon as one pair makes a mistake, either shooting the ball outside the grid or letting the pair in the middle get to the ball, that pair then goes into the middle, and the game continues. This game will help your players learn how to support each other in a team setting and begin to understand team positioning, while honing their passing skills in a fun, competitive way.

Equalizer Game   34

This game helps players concentrate on the importance of learning to move the ball on the field. Divide your players into teams of six and have them play a game. Whenever one team scores, that team can't score again until the opposing team scores. That means that the team with a goal advantage has to keep possession of the ball without trying to go for a goal. They must concentrate on supporting angles and stringing passes together and must work as a team simply to maintain possession, without the temptation of going for the goal in front of them all the time. Meanwhile, the other team is going for the equalizer, and when that team equalizes the score, both teams go back to trying to score again.

Ball Control

Keepy Up   35

Good soccer begins with good ball control. A good player must be able to receive a pass or arrest a careening ball with just a touch and then immediately resume play, with her head up and her eyes on the field. Juggling the ball in the air with the feet and other body surfaces—what we called Keepy Up in Scotland—is the most basic game for developing good touch and ball control (see the photo on page 39). The best way to introduce Keepy Up is to start with what I call one touch/one bounce. To play, the player drops the ball, touches it with the instep (where the laces of the shoe are), lets it bounce on the ground, touches it again with the instep, lets it bounce on the ground, and so on, keeping the sequence going. Once your players can handle 20 consecutive one touch/one bounce sequences, start them on a two touch/one bounce game.

Once that's mastered, take them onto the Keepy-Up Ladder. This is simply the progression when the player starts with executing 20 consecutive one touch and one bounce sequences, goes on to two touches and a bounce, three touches and a bounce, and keeps adding a touch every time, until she hits 10 bounces. If the player misses before reaching 20, she goes back to the first step on the ladder and starts climbing again.

Keepy Up is a great drill for players of any level. Some can be at one touch/one bounce, some at two touches and a bounce, and some further up the ladder. For beginners, it is a good idea to allow a bounce: it keeps the game going for a long time and lets them be successful right from the start. As players' confidence grows, you can introduce the thigh, chest, and head as alternative surfaces of control. Different parts of the foot, the inside or even the heel, can be introduced for the best players. The drill promotes confidence and is also a great doggy bag exercise for your team. As your players improve, they can begin to juggle the ball back and forth in pairs. The gradual progression in pairs play is the same: first the one touch/one bounce, then two touches, and then the ladder. And with the most advanced players, you can take out the bounce altogether.

Shooting

Straight Shots at Goal   36

For the first session of shooting at the goal, work on just straight shots. First, demonstrate a straight shot at the goal, with head down and toe pointed.

Your standing foot should be pointing toward the direction you want to hit the ball. Your striking foot follows through at the target, hitting the ball with the laces. Ask your players questions: "Which part of the foot did I use? Is my head up or down? What is my standing foot doing? Is my striking foot a wet fish?" Get them answering your questions and learning what the proper form should be.

Then divide the players into pairs and have them stand about 25 yards apart. Mark out an area for each pair, either with or without a little goal, and have them strike the ball back and forth to their partners from the ground. Remind them from time to time to keep their heads down, toes pointed. If you need to, stop the drill and demonstrate the skill again, using a player who is doing it well.

Target Shooting   37

The point of this game is to help your players gain accuracy and control while shooting at the goal. Divide the players into pairs and place them about 25 yards apart. Halfway between them, put down a cone, or even a pinny or extra ball, as a target. Each player alternates trying to shoot the ball to the target in the middle. Every time a player hits the target, he gets a point. While this cone game is going on, walk around and watch. Be sure to give plenty of praise, but at the same time help the kids who are having problems by making little corrections to fix what's not working for them.

Soccer Tennis   38

This game is great for teaching players to work on proper form when shooting. Create a minifield about 20 by 20 yards, and devise a "net" from a piece of rope draped over a couple of cones—or if rope isn't available, put up cones and pretend there is a net. Divide your players in half, with one team on one side of the net, and the other team on the other side. Have your players gently volley over the net area. If one team kicks the ball and it lands in the dead area (outside the marked playing area), it's a point for the other team. You can allow as many bounces on the ground between volleys as you like, or as the skill level of your players dictates.

Tippee-Onee   39

In this game, players must make the choice of how to field a shot: they may catch the ball as a goalkeeper, or they may try to control it with their foot and get off a quick running shot. Divide your players into pairs and have them stand approximately 25 yards apart. Each pair should have a small, six-to-seven-yard goal area at either end of their playing area. One player places the ball approximately three yards beyond her goal line and tries to score a goal on her partner. The defender is allowed one touch—or tippee—to either catch or control the ball (this is where the one tippee comes in). If she can control it with that one touch, she can then kick the ball from the point at which she stopped it, provided she doesn't go over the halfway line (approximately 12 yards). If the defender chooses to catch the ball, she drops the ball at that spot and tries to score a goal on her opponent.

Shooting Box   40

Divide your players into two teams of five players. Each team will have a goalie and two people who will play two-on-two with the other team in a 25- by 25-yard area in the middle of the field. The two remaining players will stand between the goal line and the corner flag. The players in the middle will play two-on-two for up to two minutes, getting off as many shots on goal as possible. If they kick the ball behind the goal or out of bounds, the players on the sidelines move the ball back into play, trying to get it to their teammates on the field. The ball is never out of bounds or dead; rather, it is always rebounded back into play, similar to indoor soccer or hockey.

The benefits of this game are numerous. Not only are the players in the middle working to get off as many shots as possible, but the game is also a terrific exercise for keeping all the players involved, alert to what's happening on the field, and working toward scoring for their team.

Heading

Glasgow Kisses   41

Heading is a skill that kids can be fearful about trying. As discussed in chapter 2, the best way to get them over their initial fear is to help them discover the proper technique. Start by demonstrating the skill and then ask, "Which part of your head do you strike the ball with?" Most players will respond, "Well, it's the bit without any hair." Have them take that discovery and try to repeat the same motion. Have players toss the ball up in the air and touch it gently with their heads. Eyes should be open and mouth shut. Just little touches back.

Some players will shrink into the ball, so that their heads come into their shoulders, rather than using their heads to strike out at the ball. This is where Glasgow Kisses come in. Explain that Glasgow Kisses are, literally, head butts. In this drill, have your players hold a ball standing up. First have them gently head the ball up and catch it as before. Then tell them you want them to smack the ball with a real Glasgow Kiss. Even the most timid player should respond to that.

Heading Ladder   42

Each player needs to have a ball. Have the players throw the ball into the air, head it once, and then catch it. The next time, the players should throw the ball, head it twice, and then catch it. Players should continue doing this until they can head the ball up to six times. After that, see how many times in a row they can head the ball without catching it, going for their own personal record. The key to this drill is to keep it fairly short, so that players don't get scared again and don't get sore foreheads.

You can also have your players do the Heading Ladder in pairs. Have one player throw the ball to his partner, who heads it back to him. The next time, the first player throws the ball to his partner, who heads it back to him; then the first player heads it back, and the other player catches it. Again, after about six headers, the players forget about catching the ball and see how many times they can head back and forth to each other in a row without dropping the ball.

Standing Head Game   43

Divide your players into pairs. One player throws the ball into the air and heads it to her partner without moving her feet so that all the power for the header comes from the body. The partner catches it and heads it back, also without moving her feet. Once players can do this two or three times, they should each take a step back so that they are farther apart. They should do the drill again, still without moving their feet to maximize the power coming from their bodies. When they can do the drill well from this distance, they should take another step backward. Watch to see which pair on the team can head accurately from the farthest distance.

Two-on-Two Heading   44

This is a great game for practicing heading skills. Divide your players into pairs. Each pair will defend an 8-yard-wide goal in a 10-yard-long field, which is divided in half. One player throws the ball to his partner, who heads the ball to try to score on the other goal, or heads it back to his partner to move the ball up the field closer to the goal in order to head it in. As long as the ball doesn't touch the ground, the team in possession can head the ball back and forth up the field as close to the goal as possible before trying to head it in. After a goal attempt has been made, the defending players can either catch or head the ball. If they catch the ball, then they repeat the drill—one throws the ball to the other player, who then heads it. But if they can head the ball back and it goes into the goal, that would actually count as two goals because it would be a double-header. When they opt to head the ball back to the first team, those players have the same option: either to try to catch it or to head it in for a goal. If that team heads the ball into the goal (which would be the third header), it would count as three goals.

When one team heads the ball toward the goal, the defending player may choose to head it to his teammate. The players can move up the field and try to get a little closer to the goal by making consecutive heading passes until they are right near the goal.

Rommel's Desert War   45

The object of this heading game is for one opponent to drive the other back across the field to the opposing field line. It's a fun way to practice heading between two partners. Players begin play at one end of the field, facing each other about five yards apart. One player heads the ball to her partner, who lets it bounce on the ground and then catches it. Then the receiving player, standing wherever the ball first bounced, begins the next head.

Heading Triangle   46

Divide your players into groups of three. Player number 1 throws the ball to number 2, who heads it to number 3. Then number 3 throws the ball to number 1, who heads it to number 2, who heads it to number 3. Number 3 again throws the ball to number 1, who heads it to 2, who heads it to 3, who heads it to 1, who catches it. Players should work their way up to six headers before catching the ball.

Throw-Head-Catch (Team Handball)   47

This game can be a lot of fun for more experienced players and is a great way to work on heading and teamwork skills. Divide your players into teams of four or five. Each team will have a goal to defend in a 44-yard-wide by 36-yard-long field. One team starts with the ball. A player from that team throws the ball to her teammate, who must head it to another teammate, who then catches the ball and throws it to another teammate, and so on. The team repeats the sequence of heading and throwing until they have an opportunity to score or the ball is intercepted. The point of the game is that the players alternate throws and headers—if the last ball was thrown, the next player who touches it must head the ball, even if it is an interception. If the ball hits the ground, whichever team picks it up gains possession. When the ball is headed toward the goal, everyone on the defending team can be a goalkeeper and try to catch it. But remember: when the ball is thrown at the goal, everyone must defend with their heads.

Head Tennis   48

This is a great game to promote control in heading, although it is not a game I would introduce to beginners. As the name suggests, head tennis involves heading the ball back and forth over a net or some demarcated area—cones, a bench, or a fence all work well. Initially you can allow as many bounces as you wish, and as players improve, restrict it to one bounce. The game may be played with one to six youngsters on each side.

Heading Soccer   49

This is a heading-only version of a real soccer game, played on an abbreviated field with six players on a side. Create a field no longer than 20 yards, with a goal at either end approximately 8 yards wide. Players can move the ball up the field only by heading it and can score only with a header. The goalkeeper on each team may use his hands. If the ball drops to the ground, the first team to pick it up gains possession. The only time players can use their hands is when they are picking up a dropped ball to begin heading or when playing goal.

Goalkeeping

Goal Shooting   50

Place two goals approximately 20 yards apart. Have each goalie take shots at the opposite goal, so that the other goalie can work on a variety of saves. The long distance between goals makes this drill ideal for helping the goalies make decisions about whether to catch the ball or set it up with their feet for a goal kick.

Goal Shooting with the Whole Team   51

The whole team should practice shots on goal at every practice. It can be a great exercise incorporating dribbling, passing, and shooting. Not only does it give players practice in a gamelike situation, but it also gives the goal-keeper a chance to defend lots of shots on goal in the goal that she will be defending. You can have a single line of players where the kids dribble and shoot, or two lines where they dribble, pass, and shoot. Remember to make sure players are well warmed up before shooting, which is explosive and could easily result in a pulled muscle without a proper warm-up.

This is also a great opportunity for the goalie to practice what to do after he makes the save: kick it or pass it back to a teammate, who would take it up the field in a game situation.

Attacking and Defending

Fighting Roosters   52

This game is ideal for working on ball-handling skills and for introducing how to defend the ball when an opponent is pressuring. Don't try it until your players have achieved a basic concept of ball control, or they might find the game a bit frustrating. Divide your players into pairs of similar abilities. Each player has a ball and tries to touch her partner's ball with her foot without losing control of her own ball, which she must keep moving at all times. Each time one player's ball gets touched by another player, she has to do a forfeit, say one push-up, and then the game resumes. Keep score.

This is a tremendous little game because a lot of things come out of it; one of the most important is that players learn how to handle the ball when someone is pressuring them. Don't go into all the coaching points before you start this game—just explain the rules and let them play. After your players have been at it for a while, pick out a pair who are playing the game well and have them demonstrate to the others what they have discovered. The better players will automatically stick the ball on their outside feet to keep it away from the pressure.

Then you can make some points about what's happening: "Hey, you've got the ball on the outside foot. Now can you lengthen the area. Put your arm up and out a little to protect the air around you." The next point you can make is, "Hey, can you see the pressure? Can you see your ball? Can you see the pressure?" This will help players keep their heads up. Then ask, "Hey, can you hear them? Can you feel them?" Tell them that when they use the hand nearest to the opponent, they should think of it as their radar—an early warning system. Ask them what radar does. Help them discover how to use their bodies and their sense on the field to protect the ball when they have it. Send the players back out onto the field for awhile and watch as they learn for themselves how to use their bodies as protection.

Catch the Tiger's Tail   53

This is similar to Fighting Roosters, but in this game two players play with one ball, which is the tiger's tail. The person who doesn't have possession of the ball tries to touch it with his foot—to catch the tiger's tail, while the player with the ball is trying to keep it away from his opponent. Once the ball gets touched by the player without the ball, then the player who loses the ball does a push-up, and the two players change roles. This game uses all the same principles of Fighting Roosters, including using the arm to give distance and moving the ball from the inside to the outside of the foot.

Both Fighting Roosters and Catch the Tiger's Tail help underscore the importance of getting the ball on the outside foot, the foot furthest away from the source of danger. If the defender is coming from the right, the ball would have to move to the left side of the player in possession. That player would have to have her body between the ball and the other player and be prepared to work the ball well. These games teach the player in possession to use her body as a barrier while still working on ball control—two crucial elements to the game.

Piggy in the Middle (also known as Three-on-One or Keep Ball)

This drill, described above under "Passing and Receiving," is absolutely crucial to understanding formation play. Three players form a triangle and pass the ball around a single player in the middle, who tries to intercept it. The game incorporates defenders trying to steal passes, helps your players work on *support angles*—the positions players take to allow their teammate with the ball an easy pass—and underscores the basic concepts of positions on the field. (See game 32 on page 107.)

GAMES AND DRILLS

Target Man   54

Below left. In Target Man, Xs start with the ball and look to play into an attacking player who is marked by a defender (O). The other two defenders in that area are on the goal line. If the defender wins the ball, the two players on the goal line come alive and the game reverses.

Below right. If a defender wins the ball, or if a goal is scored, players reverse their roles. In this diagram Os switch to offense while Xs drop back into defensive positions.

This game helps players learn to play in a controlled fashion in the defensive and midfield zones and then to create attacking opportunities when the ball is passed into the attacking zone. Target Man also teaches your players to make space to receive the ball.

Split the full field into an area 25 yards wide and 40 yards long. Split this again into two zones, 25 yards wide by 20 yards long, with a goal at either end. Each team has four players, with three in the defensive zone, and one attacker or "target man." One team starts the play with the ball in their defensive zone, where they play three-on-one against the other team's target man. The ball must be passed over the middle line—it can't be dribbled. Once the first team's target man has the ball, he tries to score a goal against the three defensive players on his half of the field—one who is marking the target man, one who is a general defender, and a goalkeeper. If a defender wins the ball, he plays it back to the goalkeeper, and the game becomes a three-on-one going in the reverse direction. Players should stay on their halves of the field, although more advanced teams can have one of the back players go forward and support the pass in the attacking half.

This game requires a lot of coaching, but once the players understand the concepts, the kids who can play this are well on their way to under-

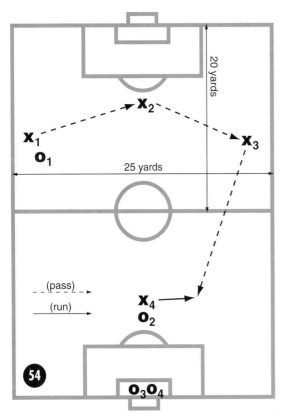

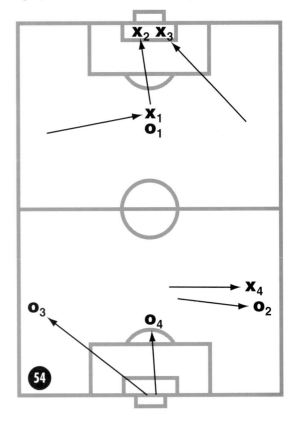

standing soccer. If they can make passes in the defensive back half of the field, even three-on-one, they are starting to understand the use of space. If they can then play the ball into the attacking area to a player who's marked, then they are showing that they are beginning to understand the need for eye contact, communication, and thinking ahead.

Two-Zone Soccer   55

This game is similar to Target Man but is played with six players on a side. The object of the game is to move the ball from defense to attack.

    Split up the field into two zones, approximately 30 yards wide by 50 yards long. You'll have two teams of six players: four defenders, including the goalkeeper, and two attackers. One goalie starts the play, and her team works the ball up the field in a four-on-two. The ball must be passed, not dribbled, over the midline, where you'll have two forwards against three defenders. The goalie is confined to the goal area. Once the ball is in the attack zone, one of the defensive players can move up and support the attack to make it a three-on-three in the attacking area. If the defenders in the attacking area gain control over the ball, then the game reverses.

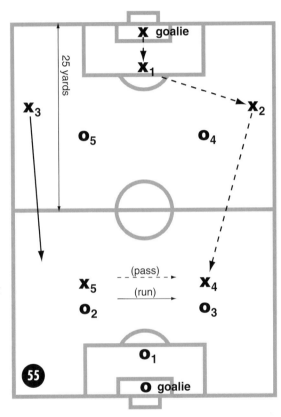

In two-zone soccer, the goalie starts the play but remains in the goal area. X passes the ball across the midline into the attacking area. Once the ball is in the attack zone, one of the defensive players (X) can move up and support the attack on a three-on-three in the attacking area.

    Another advantage to the two-zone game is that it teaches goalkeepers how to make an outlet pass, which is a pass from the goalie to a defender, wide and out to the side of the field. These are especially important for younger players, since most kids don't have the strength to kick the ball out of the scoring zone from in front of the goal.

Three-Zone Soccer   56

This game builds upon Two-Zone Soccer by introducing the third zone and lengthening the field. The field is divided into three zones that are 25 yards long by 50 yards wide. This time each team has a full squad of 16 players, eight-on-eight, with a goalkeeper, three defenders, two midfielders, and two attackers. The defenders stay in the defending third of the field, the midfielders in the midfield third, and the two attackers in the attacking third. The game is essentially an enlargement of the previous two games. Players may move from one zone to another to support the attack as the ball moves up the field, but if the ball is turned over, they immediately go back to their original positions.

Below left. In three-zone soccer, players stay in their designated zones, moving up to support the attack as the ball moves up the field. If the ball is turned over, they immediately return to their original positions.

Don't worry about offside rules in this game — just let your players get the feeling of playing from defense to midfield to attack. After a while, take away the cones marking the separate zones and let players remember their positions, where they should go, and what they should do.

Full-Field Soccer   57

Below right. In an 11-on-11 full-field game, each team has a goalkeeper, four defenders, three midfielders, and three attackers. Each zone can be marked by cones if necessary.

In this final game, you'll have a full-field, 11-on-11 game, with a goalkeeper, four defenders, three midfielders, and three attackers on each team. If you need to, you can also start out this game with the three zones marked by cones and then take them away as the game progresses. At this point the full-field rules may be introduced (see Basic Rules in chapter 2). You may also find that you'll need another team to scrimmage against, since it will require 22 players on the field at once.

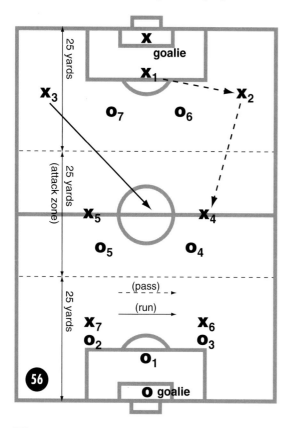

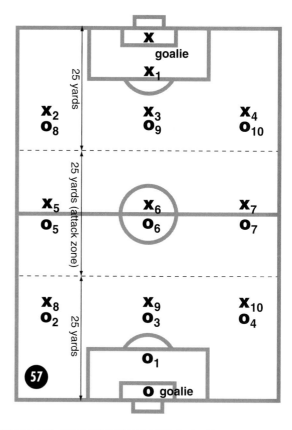

APPENDIX: Official Soccer Field Features

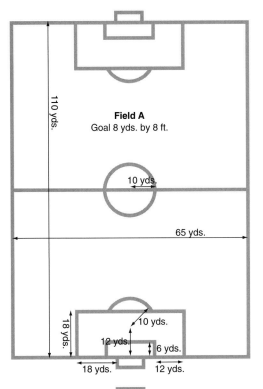

Field A
Goal 8 yds. by 8 ft.

110 yds.

10 yds.

65 yds.

18 yds.

10 yds.

12 yds.

6 yds.

18 yds.

12 yds.

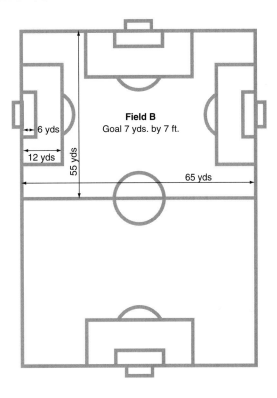

Field B
Goal 7 yds. by 7 ft.

6 yds

12 yds

55 yds

65 yds

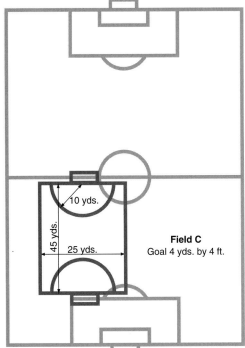

10 yds.

45 yds.

25 yds.

Field C
Goal 4 yds. by 4 ft.

Kids between the ages of 8 and 12 do best in seven-on-seven games played on scaled down fields. There are a number of ways to accommodate this (see page 21).

Referee Signals

NFHS Official Soccer Signals

Glossary

Ball control: Touching or juggling the ball.

Ball-handling: Moving with the ball.

Box: Also called *grid*; usually a square or rectangular area marked off by cones.

Centerback: Defensive player who keeps track of his opposing player in the center of the defensive end of the field.

Center circle: Circle with a 10-yard radius at the middle of the field.

Center forward: Attacking player, also known as a *striker*, who plays toward the center of the field.

Centerline: Line that divides the field in half along its width.

Center midfielder: One of three players who link together the offensive and defensive parts of a team. The center midfielder plays in the center of the field and is flanked by a left and right midfielder.

Clear: Moving the ball up the field out of scoring range, usually a long pass.

Cleats: Shoes with metal, plastic, or rubber points to provide traction.

Corner kick: Kick given to the attacking team after the defending team has played the ball over their own end line. It is taken from the corner of the end and sidelines at the side it went out.

Cover: To take up a position close to an opponent to challenge her efforts. Also, to take up a position close to a teammate to provide support.

Cross: A pass from one side of the field to either the center or the other side of the field.

Defenders: Players who usually play in front of the goal and keep the opposition forwards at bay.

Defensive zone: The opposition's half of the field.

Direct free kick: A kick awarded on a personal foul that can score directly from the kicker's foot.

Dribble: Moving with the ball, usually when a player is running past opposition players with the ball. It often involves swerving and feinting moves.

Drop ball: A means by which the referee puts the ball back into play after a temporary suspension of play when neither team is awarded possession of the ball.

Drop kick: When the ball is played on the half-volley. It is played just after it has bounced.

End line: The field boundary running along its width at each end. Also called the *goal line*.

Flank: The wide area of the field, also called the *wing*.

Forward: Players on a team responsible for most of the scoring. They play in the zone closest to the opposing goal.

Foul: A violation of the rules resulting in a free kick.

Fullback: Another word for a defender.

Goal: The ball crossing the goal line between the goal posts and the cross bar. A goal results in one point.

Goalie: The player who can pick up the ball in her team's own goal area.

Goal area: The area directly in front of the goal, 6 yards by 12 yards, from which all goal kicks are taken.

Goal kick: An indirect free kick taken by the defensive team after the ball goes out-of-bounds over the goal line having last been touched by an attacking player. The kick is taken from anywhere within the half of the goal area closer to where the ball went out of bounds.

Goal line: The out-of-bounds line at each end of the field.

Goal post: Two vertical beams 24 feet apart and 8 feet high. They form the sides of the goal and support the cross bar.

Halfback: Also called *midfielder*, the halfback plays between the defenders and the forwards.

Halftime: Intermission between two halves of the game.

Heading the ball: Striking the ball with your head.

Heads-up soccer: A good player has good vision and when in possession plays with his head up. Heads-up soccer allows the player to see the field.

Indirect free kick: A free kick that cannot score a goal unless touched by a player other than the one taking the kick.

Inside-foot pass: A pass using the inside of the foot.

Juggling the ball: Keepy-up. Keeping the ball in the air, off the ground without using your hands.

Kickoff: A player passes the ball from the center circle to a teammate to start the game or restart the game after a goal is scored.

Left back: A defensive player who keeps track of opposing players in the left area of the defensive end of the field.

Left midfielder: One of three players who link together the offensive and defensive parts of a team. The left midfielder plays on the left side of the field.

Left winger: One of two forwards who play to the sides of the striker.

Marking: Guarding an opponent.

Midfield: The middle area of the field.

Midfielders: The players who play between the defense and the attack. Another name for *halfbacks*.

Offside: A situation in which there are not two players between the furthest attacker at the moment the ball is played. One of these defenders is usually the goalkeeper, so usually a goalie plus a defender are needed to keep the attacker onside. A forward, of course, cannot be offside in her own half of the field, only on the attacking half.

One-touch passing: Restricting a player to one touch on the ball.

Out-of-bounds: A situation in which the ball crosses outside a sideline or goal line.

Outlet pass: A pass from the goalie to a defensive wingback, wide and out to the side of the field.

Passing: Moving the ball from one player on a team to another player on the same team.

Penalty area: The area, 18 yards by 44 yards, in front of the goal where the goalkeeper is permitted to use his hands.

Penalty kick: The kick taken from the penalty spot, which is 12 yards from the goal, unless otherwise directed by league rules. This is given after the defending team has committed a foul in their own penalty area (the penalty area in their defensive half). Fouls are usually for tripping, pushing, and handling the ball by players other than the goalkeeper.

Penalty spot: The small circle in front of the center of the goal line. Penalty kicks are taken from here.

Preparation touch: A touch made when a player receives a pass and readies the ball to either dribble or pass.

Punt: A ball kicked from the goalie's hands. It is not a drop kick where the ball hits the ground. In a punt, the goalie kicks the ball with her instep on the full volley.

Receiving: Getting a pass from a teammate.

Right back: A defensive player who keeps track of opposing players in the right area of the defensive end of the field.

Right midfielder: One of three players who link together the offensive and defensive parts of a team. The right midfielder plays on the right side of the field.

Right winger: One of two forwards who play to the sides of the striker.

Save: Deflection of catching of a ball by the goalkeeper to prevent a goal.

Shin guards: Pads strapped on a player's leg to protect the shins.

Shooting: Kicking the ball at an opponent's goal.

Sideline: The line running the length of the field on each side.

Soft passing: Passing using gentle, under-weighted passes.

Striker: A central attacking forward.

Striking zone: Area of attack.

Strong foot: Foot the player is most comfortable using.

Substitution: Replacement of one player on the field with another player not on the field.

Sweeper or Sweeperback: Free covering defender behind the two or three regular defenders.

Team manager: Person responsible for team's administrative and equipment needs.

Throw-In: The toss after a ball has gone out of bounds. After one team causes the ball to go out of bounds, a player from the opposing team throws the ball back in from the sideline with two hands on the ball. The ball must be thrown from behind and over the head, and both feet must remain on the ground throughout the throw.

Touchlines: Side boundaries of the field.

Trapping: Bringing the ball under control and stopping it.

Weak foot: Foot the player is least comfortable using.

Wing: Wide area of the field, also called the *flank*.

Resources

Associations and Organizations

Alliance of Youth Sports Organizations
P.O. Box 351
South Plainfield NJ 07080
E-mail: info@aoyso.com
http://www.aoyso.com/introduc.htm
AYSO is comprised of local youth sports associations whose goal is to provide high-quality and safe sports programs for young people.

American Youth Soccer Organization (AYSO)
12501 South Isis Ave.
Hawthorne CA 90250
800-872-2976
310-643-6455
Fax 310-643-5310
E-mail: webmaster@ayso.org
http://www.soccer.org
The AYSO is a national nonprofit association that establishes and maintains youth soccer programs, providing services such as coach and referee training, insurance, and tournament coordination. It has a membership of some 630,000 boys and girls aged 4½ to 18, and 250,000 volunteer coaches, referees, and administrators. Its publications include *Soccer Now*, the largest circulation soccer publication in the United States; *InPlay*, a quarterly newspaper for coaches and referees; and *Tournament Talk*, a monthly listing of AYSO Tournaments.

National Clearinghouse for Youth Sports Information (NCYSI)
800-688-5437 (KIDS)
http://nays.org/ncysi.html
NCYSI offers both an online and print catalog of books, instructional videos, and other resources related to youth sports.

National Soccer Coaches Association of America (NSCAA)
6700 Squibb Road, Suite 215
Mission KS 66202
800-458-0678
913-362-1747
Fax 913-362-3439
http://www.nscaa.com
NSCAA is the largest single-sport coaching association in the world, with more than 15,000 members. The NSCAA provides educational clinics,

academies, and seminars. It publishes the bimonthly *Soccer Journal* and offers diploma courses in all 50 states.

National Youth Sports Coaches Association (NYSCA)
800-729-2057
E-mail: nysca@nays.org
http://www.nays.org/nysca.html#new
NYSCA trains volunteer coaches in all aspects of working with children and athletics. In addition to training, coaches receive continuing education and insurance coverage and subscribe to a coaching code of ethics.

National Youth Sports Officials Association (NYSOA)
800-729-2057
E-mail: officials@nays.org
http://www.nays.org/nysoa.html
NYSOA trains volunteer youth sports officials, providing them with information on the skills required, fundamentals of coaching, as well as common problems they may encounter.

National Youth Sports Safety Foundation (NYSSF)
http://www.nyssf.org
NYSSF is a nonprofit, educational organization whose goal is to reduce the risks of sports injury to young people.

North American Youth Sports Institute
http://www.naysi.com/
NAYSI's website features information and resources to help teachers, coaches, and other youth leaders, including parents, interact more effectively with children around sports. It includes a resource section that lists books on sports and coaching, as well as two interactive sections that give a browser an opportunity to submit questions on fitness, recreation, and sports. The website's newsletter, Sport Scene, focuses on youth programs.

Parents Association for Youth Sports (PAYS)
http://www.nays.org/pays.html
PAYS provides materials and information for youth sports programs to help teach parents about their roles and responsibilities in children's sports activities.

START SMART Sports Development Program
800-729-2057, 561-684-1141
Fax 561-684-2546
E-mail: startsmart@nays.org
http://www.nays.org/startsmart.html

START SMART is designed to teach parents how to best help their children develop the motor skills necessary for a successful start in sports.

U.S. Youth Soccer Association (USYSA)
899 Presidential Drive, Suite 117
Richardson TX 75081
800-4-SOCCER
http://www.usysa.org
U.S. Youth Soccer is a national nonprofit body of over 600,000 volunteers and administrators and over 300,000 coaches, most of whom also are volunteers. U.S. Youth Soccer registers over 3 million youth players between the ages of 5 and 19 and organizes state, regional, and national tournaments.

Programs

Adapted Physical Education
E-mail: pec@vt.edu
This section of PE Central (see above) offers information to help teachers of physically challenged students. The site suggests many ways to modify sports and activities to make them accessible to all students. In soccer, for example: substitute walking for running; have well-defined boundaries and reduce playing area; play six-a-side soccer; allow wheelchair-bound students to keep the ball on their laps; use a target that makes noise when hit; use a deflated, brightly colored, nerf, or beeper ball.

PE Central
http://pe.central.vt.edu/
This website for physical education teachers, students, and parents is designed to provide the most current information on appropriate physical education programs, helping young people on their way to a lifetime of physical fitness and health.

Electronic Newsletters

Coaching Youth Sports
http://www.chre.vt.edu/~/cys/
Virginia Tech's Health and Physical Education program sponsors this website, which provides coaches, athletes, and parents with general, rather than sport-specific, information about skills for youth. The site also allows browsers to submit questions.

Sports Parents
http://www.sportsparents.com/
Sports Parents provides a variety of articles from the magazine *Sports Parents*, a supplement to *Sports Illustrated for Kids*. Topics include coaching, sportsmanship, nutrition and fitness, equipment, sports medicine and safety, and finance and travel. A parents' tips section covers issues such as winning and losing, sibling rivalry, helping a child cope with frustration, and self-esteem.

Youth Sports Network
http://www.ysn.com/
Youth Sports Network is a multifaceted site with a featured sport of the week, news stories about youth sports, and a directory of sports camps. An instructional page covering soccer, basketball, baseball, and softball offers tips and ideas for both players and coaches. The site also offers information on exercise, nutrition, and first aid.

Index

About the Author

Bobby Clark is currently Director of Soccer at Stanford University, where he oversees, directs, and helps set the philosophy for the university's soccer programs. As the men's team coach, he took Stanford all the way to the 1998 NCAA Championship game, losing to Indiana in the NCAA final.

A 1967 graduate of Jordanhill College, Clark has had a wide, varied, and successful career as both a player and a coach. He played from 1962 until 1982 in the Scottish League, with 17 years and 696 first-team games for Aberdeen. During that period he was capped 17 times for the Scottish National team and was part of their squad in the 1970, 1974, and 1978 World Cup campaigns.

He also enjoyed two spells in the U.S. professional league when he came across in the Scottish off-season and played for the Washington Whips in 1967 and San Antonio Thunder in 1976.

A Scottish "A" license coach and a Scottish Football Association staff coach, he spent his last five years as a player with Aberdeen, doubling as a youth coach. He helped develop some of the players who were to make Aberdeen the top club side in Europe. From Aberdeen he went to Africa, where he spent a year as Director of Coaching with the Bulawayo Highlanders, one of Zimbabwe's top club sides. At this time he had the fascinating challenge of coaching the club's U-14, U-16, U-18, and Senior teams.

From Africa, Clark came to the United States and spent nine happy years at Dartmouth College, where he won three Ivy League titles and twice advanced to the quarter-finals of the NCAA Championships. He was twice named Region I "Coach of the Year" and propelled Dartmouth into the NCAA top-ten ranking during each of his last five seasons.

In 1994, he left Dartmouth and headed down under to New Zealand as National Coach, where he coached that country's U-17s, U-20s, and Olympic U-23s, as well as their Senior National squad. He spent two successful years in Kiwi land, where he was awarded the 1995 Jim McMullen Trophy as the person who did the most for New Zealand soccer in that year.

On returning to the United States in 1996, Clark was approached by Ted Leland to take over the position of Director of Soccer at Stanford. In his three years on the Farm, he has twice taken them to the NCAA tournament and was voted Far West Coach of the Year in 1997.

Clark's love of the game runs in his family: Son Jamie, a Stanford graduate and two-time All-American, now plays in the MLS for the San Jose Clash. Daughter Jennifer, a Dartmouth graduate, served as an assistant coach at Dartmouth, Stanford, and William & Mary before becoming head coach at Christopher-Newport University. Tommy, a Dartmouth graduate, was a regional All-American who played professionally for the New Mexico Chiles before returning to Dartmouth to pursue studies in medicine.

Clark and his wife, Bette, live in Stanford, California.